The Mary Experiment

When DOING and BEING Collide

DIANNE DEATON VIELHUBER

The Mary Experiment:
Challenging Busy Marthas to Sit at Jesus' Feet

All scriptural notations are taken from the Holy Bible.
Scriptural quotations marked CEB are from the Common English Bible.
Scriptural quotations marked CEV are from the Contemporary English Version.
Scriptural quotations marked TLB are from the Living Bible.
Scriptural quotations marked NCB are from the New Century Version.
Scriptural quotations marked NIV are from the New International Version.
Scriptural quotations marked NLT are from the New Living Translation.
Scriptural quotations marked NRSV are from the New Revised Standard Version.

ISBN 978-1-73402280-0-7

A Special Invitation from Dianne

If you are a person who struggles with too many things going on in your life, *The Mary Experiment* is designed for you. Each chapter includes Reflection Questions and a Prayer. To dig even deeper, please go to https://upbeat-writer-402.ck.page/36c55012ba and download the free *Journal and Reflection Questions* PDF. This Journal is designed to help you examine your own life and encourage you to begin your own Mary Experiment. Whether you study this book by yourself, with an accountability partner(s), or as a group book study, the Journal provides additional questions, reflections and opportunities for you to embrace the concepts articulated in *The Mary Experiment*.

For more spiritual encouragement and reflection, please sign-up to receive my blogs at www.SimpleWordsofFaith.com. Share your own spiritual journey in the Simple Words of Faith group on Facebook. I look forward to meeting you regularly there!

Would you like a daily prayer as you begin your day? Text simplewordsoffaith to 33222. Every day, you will receive a free daily prayer text to help center you in the Spirit of God.

What others say about the daily prayer text:

When I wake up in the morning, I look forward to my daily devotional text message. It sets my mood for the day and inspires me. I enjoy being able to look back at it throughout the day during challenging or reflective times. I am able to see devotions from today to two weeks ago for my reference to help inspire me in whatever I may be facing. This has been truly a blessing in my life to help reset my focus on God throughout each day. - Liz Nelson

It is a blessing every morning to receive a devotional text message from Dianne. It is a 7 a.m. wake up call which I look forward to. Frequently, it is like she can 'see' my needs - looking into my soul. Sending a thoughtful message just for me. Something to think about throughout the day. - Rhoda Barden

Dedication

This book is dedicated to my husband, whom I affectionately refer to as Hubby Rick. Thanks for encouraging me to follow my dream and let it come to life through the pages of this book. You have unconditionally loved this recovering Martha in the most gracious of ways. Most importantly, thanks for encouraging me to be the Christian God calls me to be. You will always be my Sweetie Pea!

XOXO -
PD

Contents

The Story

While Jesus and his disciples were traveling, Jesus entered a village where a woman named Martha welcomed him as a guest. She had a sister named Mary, who sat at the Lord's feet and listened to his message. By contrast, Martha was preoccupied with getting everything ready for their meal. So, Martha came to him and said, "Lord, don't you care that my sister has left me to prepare the table all by myself? Tell her to help me."

The Lord answered, "Martha, Martha, you are worried and distracted by many things. One thing is necessary. Mary has chosen the better part. It won't be taken away from her."

- Luke 10:39-42 (CEB)

INTRODUCTION

The Talk

It was NOT what I wanted to hear.

For 19 years, my professional occupation had been serving as a pastor. When teaching and sharing messages, I often encouraged people to live the life they want. A life which focuses on the things most important to them. A life with few, or even *no*, regrets at the end.

I know who God is in my life. I practice my faith. I accomplish countless tasks. But contentment is missing. A peace that passes all understanding is mostly at bay. 'Joy-filled' isn't exactly how I would describe my daily life.

At the beginning of summer in 2017, my husband, whom I affectionately refer to as Hubby Rick, shared a simple request. He wanted to eat lunch and go for a walk together a couple times a week. A reasonable request, right?

As important as I would like to say this was, I did not hold up my end of the deal. By mid-summer, I had only fulfilled Rick's request once or twice.

After supper one July evening, I suggested we go for a walk. During the first 17+ years of our marriage, Rick and I did not see each other every day. We saw each other only a few days a week. As a multi-tasker, I envisioned this walk would provide time for us to catch up on the week's happenings.

The previous days had been difficult. One of the churches I was serving at the time was the victim of a $20,000 internet scam - over one-quarter of this church's annual budget. Every waking moment of my life felt consumed with managing this challenge. Add in a funeral and extra work for my part-time non-church job, and I was near my limit.

Our conversation began with me sharing thoughts related to the internet scam. Mid-rant, Rick abruptly stopped walking. He looked me squarely in the eyes and asked me when I was going to get my act together. When would I focus on doing the things *we* talk about accomplishing, but he ends up doing on his own because I don't prioritize the time? When would the things I say are the 'most important' truly become my top priorities? When would I be available for something other than work?

Whew. That wasn't the talk I had in mind.

I am a recovering over-committer. Historically, I have had little ability to say "no" to an immediate need... unless it related to my own personal care. Caring for those most important to me often slid down the list as well. While I yearned for "balance" in my life, I had lost all ability to have a clear understanding of what balance was.

This was not something new for me. I have struggled with this since as far back as I can remember. As a young child, I knew there were more choices of what I *could* do, than I would have the opportunity to complete. I purposefully designed my life to try and do it ALL. I have mastered the art of knowing just enough about a multitude of things to make me dangerous. Although this has often served me well, I am consistently over-extended. I have prepared and led a funeral service; printed and folded the worship bulletins; made the luncheon sandwiches; played the special music; and conducted a meaningful graveside service... all for the same loved one. Typically, I'm tired and exhausted - but at least I am never bored!

At the time of my most recent zero-ending birthday, I mentally took stock and evaluated my life and priorities. While some parts of my life were OK, others felt completely out-of-sync. I longed to experience a deeply devoted life to God, using my very best gifts and talents for the glory of God's kingdom. My core yearned to know that what I do makes a difference.

Some people may look at me and think that was already what I was doing. My heart said something different. I felt like a car with 200,000 miles on it - in working condition, but *well* used. A little rust here and there, with parts showing age. I have burned through lots of tires, and the current ones are bald. They might explode if another unexpected pothole appears. It is an

OK car. But is "OK" good enough in this journey of life?

A biblical story that resonates with my life is Luke 10:38-42. Jesus is in Bethesda visiting siblings Mary and Martha. During the years of Jesus' full-time ministry, He developed a close relationship with these sisters and their brother, Lazarus (Yes, *that* Lazarus). On this visit, we observe Martha scurrying around the house, entertaining house guests. Her guests' feet are properly cleaned upon arrival. She makes fresh hummus and offers just-pressed olive oil for dipping warm, fresh bread. Guests sit on comfortable pillows in the appropriate pecking order from Jesus. With water to haul in, wine to decant, candles to light and a whole host of other duties, this hostess with the mostest has an endless to-do checklist.

We feel the tension of Martha doing ALL the work while her apparently lazy sister, Mary, ignores her. I can hear Martha huffing to herself, "How can Mary have the audacity to just sit there? Can't she see there is so much to do? Why isn't she helping me?"

Martha's frustration escalates. Did she try to address Mary privately? We do not know. Our front-row seat comes when Martha takes her complaint all the way to the top: to Jesus. She pursues "the talk" with Jesus.

For those of us who are "doers," we have empathy for Martha. Jesus' response would have shocked us too. He turns Martha's world upside down when He honors Mary for simply sitting at His feet and hanging onto every word He says. I hear Jesus chuckling as He tells Martha to take a chill pill and stop worrying about whether the silver has been properly polished or not. "Instead, come sit with me," Jesus says. "Only this is really important."

We do not know how Martha responded. But it cannot have been fun to be the receiver of Jesus' stinging words. How does she handle this reprimand? Is Martha able to relax and enjoy the dinner party or does she stomp out of the room, even more upset with Jesus than with Mary?

My soul stung after "the talk" with Hubby Rick. My guess is that Martha's soul did not expect Jesus' response, just as my soul was not anticipating Rick's reply. As I read Martha's story, I wanted to reach out, grab her hand and say, "Oh, I *so* know how you feel, sister!"

I have been 100% Martha nearly all my life. I am in all things a doer. "Being" is rarely part of my day. Repeatedly, I catch myself looking at my watch, trying to figure out how I can squeeze six hours of work into the next three hours. Can I get this week's sermon finished before making supper? Answer some of the e-mails looming in my inbox? Will there be time to write a blog today? Can I balance the checkbook while ordering a book for next week's study?

The world needs Martha's. Martha's get things done. Martha's change companies, make churches flourish, have great intentions for their families, and desire to leave the world a better place than before their tornado of activity arrived. They accomplish more before noon than some people tackle in a week. We admire their commitment and dedication and praise them for their unending bag of tricks.

Living with a Martha can be exhausting. They seldom find daily joy because they are so focused on what is next, they forget to celebrate any big or small win. They never quite feel content. They find it nearly impossible to savor the here and now because they are checking off the next three things they must act on before the end of the day.

Do you ever feel like this? Or is it just me?

Based on the people I interact with, I think there are lots of Martha's in this world. Words like "burnt out," "exhausted," and "stressed" get thrown around like candy at a parade. 'Doing' Martha's find little space to contemplate how a 'being' Mary might live. My life has been filled with endless to-do lists - things that *should* be done. Too often, I am a swirl of commotion that makes people jump out of the way as I come charging through. My efficient, detail-oriented Martha attitude seldom lets the deeply-buried Mary, yearning for quiet and peace, escape her well-hardened shell.

People need space to just "be," without constantly "doing." I speak of this during worship. I have written blogs about this. I have promised myself that, next week, I'll find time to just be. While I accepted this in theory, application usually evaded me. My well-used car needs an oil change, a tune-up, and a new set of tires... yesterday. It also needs a break.

If you have a hard time saying, "No," I empathize. When you feel guilty about relaxing rather than tackling one more thing on your to-do list, I know your pain. While contentment and joy often seem unrealistic, they can be in more abundance than many of us experience on a daily basis.

"The talk" brought me back to my need to revisit whether being a Martha 24/7 is best for me, my marriage, my health, and my sanity. I had been toying with the concept of a "Mary Experiment" for a while. I wanted to see if Martha's like me could add some Mary-ness into their lives. I had tried this before, but this time, I wanted it to be different. This time, I would make it *personal.* I would commit to doing more than just thinking about how to live a Mary Experiment in my life. I would seriously reflect upon my previous life experiences, examine the choices I made, and make myself vulnerable by documenting my journey towards becoming a recovering Martha.

The Mary Experiment is my attempt to discover ways to embody more Mary in my life. Did you pick up this book because you are a struggling Martha who longs for a minute of Mary in your life? Consider the words on these pages as part of "the talk" that might encourage you to pursue a little less *doing*, and a little more *being*, in your daily life.

As you read *The Mary Experiment,* I encourage you to make this journey personal. Create your own Mary Experiment. At the end of each chapter, there are reflection questions. Read them and contemplate or journal your answers. Use the free downloadable journal to guide you through your own experiment. Find another person with whom to share your answers. Take time to read this book. Savor the words. Breathe at the end of a difficult sentence. Underline a phrase that catches your attention. Star a favorite paragraph.

As a recovering Martha, I promise to be honest and vulnerable with my experience. I pray something in my story connects with your story. This book does not have a fine-tuned, step-by-step process of how to quickly shift a person's life from running in Martha mode to a more contemplative Mary mode. I have tried this pattern for 40 years and failed miserably every time. This book takes us on a journey of committing to see if making small changes in daily living allows more space to just "be," instead of constantly "doing." My prayer is that through the process, we will find more joy, contentment and peace.

Countless times, I have wished my younger self would have been slightly open to the concept of a Mary Experiment. Delaying my Mary Experiment only delayed the discovery of living a life embracing the values I desired.

Rick's sharp remarks did not ruin our walk that evening. His questions allowed for a more serious discussion. After "the talk," did I magically and immediately change everything? Unfortunately, no. I knew that I needed to make changes. It would take time to get where I longed to be. It would involve major revamping. But it was also time.

I yearn to sit around a campfire without making a list in my head of what I should be doing. I dream of enjoying the beautiful wrap-around porch on our house as a Sabbath spot with no guilt or shame. I long to have lunch and walk with my husband several days a week. I pray we can tackle the list of things we yearn to do together.

If you are a doing-Martha who dreams of more joy, contentment, and peace in your life, please join me on this journey. Together, let us explore how we can become recovering Martha's.

Part 1:

The Tension Between Martha & Mary

Chapter 1

Mary & Martha's Story

The Lord answered, "Martha, Martha, you are worried and distracted by many things. One thing is necessary. Mary has chosen the better part. It won't be taken away from her."

- Luke 10:41-42 (CEB)

Early in the process of beginning my Mary Experiment, my Mom passed away. While my siblings and I knew this could happen any time, the timing was profound. I had just decided to take "the talk" to heart. I had pulled the trigger on making significant changes. Yet, as I was attempting to create a true Mary Experiment in my life, my world shifted.

The previous four years had been a whirlwind. I had served two churches on an interim basis. While technically "part-time," I regularly logged more than full-time hours. I also worked a part-time marketing job. I constantly felt inadequate in trying to juggle these two professional responsibilities.

In the middle of this four-year stint, Hubby Rick and I moved. We purchased a 110-year-old Victorian farmhouse that needed a complete overhaul. Initially, we moved our possessions into two rooms and "camped" for five months while we updated half of the house. In great Martha fashion, less than 48 hours before a Christmas Open House, dishes found homes in the kitchen cupboards for the first time. Two days later, over 120 people "oohed" and "aahed" at our renovated house. Most did not see the part of the house where one could barely walk.

In those same years, Rick and I provided care for my father-in-law, helped with our grandchildren, continued to remodel our property and transitioned my mom through moves and major downsizing. Meanwhile, we both worked more than full-time jobs. While I felt overwhelmed at the time, I did not believe that I could step back from any of these commitments. I did not want to let anyone down, myself included. My life was a hot mess.

Could I apply the brakes to my 90-miles-an-hour life?

A few weeks after "the talk," I submitted my resignation to the two churches. I explained my intention of designing a Mary Experiment, which I would document and compile into a book. In sharing my heart's yearnings with others, I felt committed to follow through with this experiment.

Yet even the best laid plans can be interrupted. A couple weeks after my last day with the churches, my 81-year-old mom's health changed. She lived in a nursing home. This was not her choice, and happened only after several cycles of falling, recovering in a nursing home, moving back to an apartment with additional help, and then falling again.

The transition to the nursing home had been difficult. Why? Because my Mom was a Martha. Fiercely independent, she made her own decisions and had spent most of her life taking care of other people. She did not like, nor want, to be dependent upon others, and regularly reminded my siblings and me of this.

It was hard to watch as my mom's body and mind could no longer do the things she willed them to do. After a lifetime of "doing," transitioning to a life of "being" was against her nature. Just before Christmas, she fell again. This time, it was clear her ability to rebound was not possible. My siblings and I implemented steps that would allow Mom to live her last days peacefully, with dignity, and as comfortably as possible. Before she passed away, we had opportunities to say good-bye, and prepare our hearts for life without parents.

On a very snowy January day, we celebrated Mom's life. The surrounding schools had canceled because of significant snowfall the previous evening. My phone received messages from friends opting not to drive several hours in less-than-ideal Wisconsin winter conditions to attend the service. So, I was very surprised when our dear friends Robin and Rhonda walked into the church. They had braved the weather to be with us. Rick and I were overwhelmed with gratitude.

During the service, I shared how my Mom was independent, hard-working, and determined. She was a typical farmwife: sewed our clothes, canned and froze food, and led 4-H. She made lard, cooked down maple syrup, and taught us how to make homemade ice cream. She worked daily on the farm: fed animals, ran farm equipment, and handled the bookwork. As our taxi driver, Mom drove my siblings and me to church, school, 4-H, FFA, and youth activities. Whether it was a sporting event, a concert, a speaking contest, or the fair, Mom seldom missed our activities. Every birthday, she made our choice of special cookies or cupcakes for our entire class. She made thousands of the famous Deaton Santa Claus cookies, each with special decorations and piped frosting. Mom lived her faith in God and was actively involved in a local church.

When our family farm felt the financial squeeze of the early 1980's, Mom worked off the farm to provide more income. Somehow, she still worked on the farm too, and kept up with all her kid's activities. There were many nights she slept very little.

Mom also thought of others. At Christmas, she lovingly baked homemade bread and gave it to the milkman, postman, neighbors, and others. She invited people with no holiday plans to our family celebrations, where they were treated like family.

My mom taught me many, many things. I learned how to juggle multiple commitments and activities. During the memorial service, I was brutally honest when I shared that Mom had highly influenced my Martha-like tendencies. In fact, my parents had raised four Martha-like children.

After the memorial service, we retreated to the church basement for lunch. Rick and I sat next to Robin and Rhonda. I had not put a forkful of food into my mouth before Rhonda said, "Now I know exactly why you are the way you are. As you spoke about your mom today, I kept thinking that you weren't talking about her. You were talking about yourself."

It can be very hard to hear the most obvious of statements. Rhonda was right. Many traits and habits I embody were learned via osmosis from my mom. It was not easy to tell the difference from Mom's story and my story. Like my mom, I never felt that I had an alternative option. Living as a Martha was just what we did.

Where did my mom learn how to be a Martha? Simply by watching her own mother. I am confident this lifestyle was passed down from generation to generation through my mom's maternal family. It was a foundation of how my ancestors were raised and lived. I was the next woman to carry out these attributes.

Losing my mom cemented the necessity for me to reflect more about my Martha life. While we ate hot sandwiches and ice cream (a favorite of Mom's), the realization of Rhonda's words sunk in. Reflecting upon wanting more Mary-ness in my life *must* become a high priority.

Mary and Martha's Story

We may call this passage of scripture from Luke's gospel "Martha's story." I could also call this "Ann's story" (my mom's name), or "Dianne's story." Maybe you can call this "My story."

When we call this "Martha's story," we leave out an important component. It is also "Mary's story." According to Jesus, if we only observe Martha's contribution, we drop an important part of the storyline.

As I explored this story with other people, I received a variety of responses. They include:

- The world needs Martha's. Otherwise, who will get anything done?
- What's wrong with being a Martha?
- Shouldn't Jesus have acknowledged all that Martha did for him?
- I know too many Mary's in my life. Someone must be Martha.

For years, I defended my Martha attitude. I felt Martha got a bad rap for being a take-charge woman who was not afraid to get things done. Is this such a bad thing? Don't we encourage our children and grandchildren to dream big and go after their goals?

I often have felt it would be helpful to know more of Martha's situation. Was she a busy-body by choice, or out of necessity? Did someone model this way of living to Martha? Martha's house did not have an electric or gas stove, nor a dishwasher or refrigerator. There wasn't a food processor to mash the garbanzo beans for hummus, or a mixer to incorporate the bread ingredients together. There wasn't a deli to run to for last minute items, or a pizza delivery service when unexpected company showed up. Running a first-century kosher Jewish household took a lot of work, especially if your sister didn't assist.

There is a palpable tension between being 100% Martha and 100% Mary. Neither extreme is best. Having some Martha and some Mary allows us to get things done and change people's lives, while at the same time keeping us close to God's heart and God's will for our lives.

Most people naturally lean towards being either a Martha or a Mary. Moving from one personality (doing vs. being) to the other is not a simple shift. Is it fair to ask a person to change, when maybe this is how they are wired? Do some Martha's become resentful when they want to be a Mary, but feel the opportunity is not available to them?

Should the Martha's of the world deem that embodying some Mary in their lives would be a good idea? Yes, because Jesus told Martha that she was missing the one and most important thing. When we ignore Jesus' calling to live with some Mary in our lives, we are no different than Ms. Busy-ness Martha herself.

After my mom's death, my friend Kristi sent me a card. She didn't know Mom. Yet, her words accurately described her:

> *Like most of our moms, I'm sure she also secretly wore a Wonder Woman costume every day with everything she could get accomplished in a single bound. From taking care of the family, helping on the farm, being involved in the community, and at the end of the day, have a fabulous meal prepared. She had to be so proud of the strong, caring woman you have become and the ease at which you can do so many things in a professional way. I hope you are at peace and the memories you share with family and friends help you through this difficult time.*

Huge tears rolled down my cheeks as I read Kristi's words. She captured my mom so clearly. She also accurately articulated the internal struggle I feel every day.

Finding an appropriate mix between Martha and Mary-ness seems to be a crux for many people. How can the Martha's of the world empower their lives for Mary moments? Can Martha's allow themselves to move towards Mary-ness, while still keeping the admirable aspects of their personalities?

Altering my story to include more Mary moments in my life began with making the commitment to myself that I *wanted* to change my story. In my head, I knew that I was missing out on the one and most important thing in my life. Lip service to change my priorities would not be enough. This could no longer be something I "should do."

Shifting my life would require making hard choices in my heart. If I wanted to write a different ending to the story I was living, I needed to choose whether action would happen. Was I willing to take small, significant steps and change the deep-seeded Martha tendencies in my life? Would I be able to release control of the many things I "do" and allow myself opportunities to "be?"

How do you want your story to end? Are you content with the current status of Martha and Mary mix in your life? Or, do you yearn for something different? Have you allowed yourself to embrace the one and important thing in your life?

Reflection Questions:

1. Who is someone that has modeled Martha-like tendencies for you? How do you specifically see their influence in how you live your life?

2. Ask a trusted friend to identify your Martha and Mary tendencies. When are your Martha attitudes helpful? When are they challenging? How have you incorporated Mary's attitude into your life?

3. Do you struggle with Mary's lack of help to Martha in this story? If so, what bothers you the most about this?

Prayer:

Dear God – You have designed each one of us in a powerfully unique and special way. While You call each one of us Your Own, no two of us are alike. Thank you for creating us to each be our own special person. Thank you for bringing powerful role models into our lives. May we not be afraid to continue to be molded and shaped by You. Amen.

CHAPTER 2

It Started Not with Martha, but with Helen

But Martha was distracted by her many tasks ...

- Luke 10:40a (NRSV)

Martha and I have been pals for as long as I can remember, even before I knew her story. A significant influencer in my life, I was oblivious to how deeply she is tucked into every corner of my personality.

I lived a Martha lifestyle for years before I knew there was a biblical character who embodied my daily existence. After we formally met, she turned my life upside down. Unaware that my life had needed to be righted, I wasn't quite sure what to do with her. Many more years passed before I embraced the opportunity to tweak and adjust my Martha attitude.

Before I met Martha, I lived the way my parents taught me to live. I grew up in a household in which not doing your best was frowned upon. Life was defined by working hard and giving it your all. Slackers weren't allowed. When challenges came along, you dug a little deeper and kept on going. Quitting was not an option.

Until the time my parents had no choice.

My parents moved from Iowa to Wisconsin in the early 1960's. They operated a Wisconsin dairy farm for over 25 years. In the late 1980's, American agriculture went through a ridiculously challenging time. Interest rates sky-rocketed. Producers who had been encouraged to expand their operations in the 1970's and early 1980's faced unsustainable debt. For years, my parents lived Martha-like lives as they tried to hang on to the family farm.

Even after liquidating all the assets they could, they still were unable to make the ever-growing massive interest payments. They were emotionally, mentally, physically, and spiritually exhausted. Finally, my parents had to let the farm go back to the bank.

While it was hard to see my parents give up the farm, they *didn't* give up on life. They pursued new careers and began to dig themselves out of a deep financial hole.

My parents moved into the town where my siblings and I had graduated from high school. With only 2,000 residents, it was the type of idyllic American small town where you get to know your neighbors. For us, that was Helen and Alfred. Although a generation older than my parents, these retired dairy farmers quickly established a strong neighborly bond. Our family celebrated holidays with Alfred and Helen. Recipes were exchanged. If a sick house cat or orphan lamb needed looking in on, Helen graciously walked across the lawn in her 1950's-style house dress and sturdy shoes to tend to the animal. When Mom's house ran out of guest bedrooms, Helen's cottage-like bungalow provided overflow sleeping quarters.

Helen passed away while I was attending my first semester of seminary. In great Martha-like fashion, I completed the last exam of the semester just in time to drive to Helen's service. In a message entitled, "Helen and Martha and Mary," Rev. Kangas interlaced the story of Martha and Mary with Helen's life. He appreciated Helen's appropriate mix of Martha and Mary characteristics. Nodding to Martha, he was confident there were enough cookies in Helen's freezer for the funeral luncheon. None of the church ladies would have had to prepare their favorite recipes. Yet, when someone stopped at Helen's house unannounced, life paused. She pulled out her prettiest dishes, brewed a steaming pot of coffee, and sat and listened. Helen designed her life with the appropriate tension of having just enough Martha to be prepared, while also tending to the soul of her and other's spiritual garden.

Sitting in the pew during Helen's service, I came to the grim reality that I had very little Mary in my life. The even grimmer reality was that in the 30+ years of my life at this point, I had experienced only glimpses of Mary. As a child, I rode bike, read books, and played with my sisters. These were relished moments. In our family, the unspoken mantra was that hard work was never a dirty word. My sisters and I were involved in daily chores and responsibilities on the farm, as well as in the house. This is what my mom did. This is what we all did.

My dad told me that I could do anything I wanted to do, if I worked hard enough. His encouragement had nothing to do with being smart enough or skilled enough. It was rooted in a deep work ethic and not giving up. Ever. This was why it had been so difficult for my parents to let the farm go.

At the time of Helen's service, my life was full and getting fuller. I was attending seminary full time. Soon, I began pastoring two small churches located two hours from school. I had never been a pastor, and did not know how to "be" a pastor. I continued to work another part-time job to support myself and the unending seminary expenses. In a few days, I moved into a rented apartment. My life felt like a bellowing car flying down a rural country road, leaving a flurry of dust behind. Every day, I gripped the steering wheel, trying to keep the car on the road and not end up flipped-over in the ditch.

I had so little understanding of what it meant to be a Mary. I could only identify one time in my life when I had intentionally allowed for Mary time. It was during one school year when I lived overseas as a missionary in the former Soviet Union republic of Kazakhstan. Finally, I had time to read, journal and reflect. Upon returning to the United States, I willed myself to continue these disciplines. But reading the obnoxious number of books each week for seminary or completing the latest paper took higher priority. Relaxation was going for a 20-minute walk or run, possibly a hurried meal with a friend.

I felt like the message at Helen's funeral was intended for me. My mind explored new questions. What does a Mary life look like? How does a person balance earning a living, supporting family, enjoying friends, and favorite passions and hobbies, while still spending quality time with God? Was it even possible to have Mary-time in my over-extended Martha life?

I lacked a way to articulate how I felt, until Martha and Mary showed up at Helen's funeral. Countless times, I willed myself not to take on anything new. I would create a healthier work schedule, prioritize nurturing my spiritual soul, and take better care of myself physically as well as those close to my heart. This declaration usually lasted less than 24 hours. The seemingly urgent and necessary phone call or email request always took precedence.

I developed tricks to keep an ever-growing number of balls in the air. Letting one drop would be unacceptable. If something was not coming together, I would swoop in at the last minute and take care of things. The show would go on with seemingly no hiccups or blunders.

I was overly prideful of my ability to pull something together with any small amount of time or dedicated resources. I strapped on my big-girl pants and made sure things came together. After doing this for years, I had no concept of letting something fail. "Dianne to the rescue!" was my silent mantra. The adrenaline rush of making sure everything would be just right fueled my tired soul. I proudly wore the unofficial badges of being professional, particular, and present - if only for my own observance. I would not disappoint others or myself.

Hubby Rick's main love language is quality time together. Early in our marriage, we were more proactive about finding that time. We'd squeeze in a bike ride or a short day-trip. Eventually, I started bowing out because I felt stretched by an endless "to-do" list of my own making. I had no clue how to live without constant busy-ness in my life. I proudly declared that sleeping was something I could do after I died.

Do you see similar patterns in your story? What "things" have fueled your Martha-like tendencies? Where are you prideful about your abilities and commitments?

Acknowledging Martha in Your Life

At Helen's funeral service, I realized that an out-of-control Martha life was NOT standard for everybody. Driving home, it rained and rained. The wipers could not keep up with the huge water drops splattering on the car's windshield. My life felt like the wipers: so many things raining down and no ability to keep up. How had my life gotten so out of control? Soon, I would be adding the responsibility of serving as the pastor for two churches. How crazy was I?

Like my post-farming parents, could I give up my Martha-like existence without giving up on life?

Every night before I go to bed, I plug my cell phone in for recharging. Heaven forbid I start the day without a fully charged phone! But how many days do I begin a day not fully recharged physically, emotionally, mentally, or spiritually?

Most often, I begin the day already tired from a lack of quality sleep. I feel defeated by an unending to-do list that grows throughout the day, rather than feeling life is manageable. As the day drags on, I am a phone that is running too many apps simultaneously, each sucking the energy out of me. I have no concept that every once in a while, I need to "close all open apps." I convince myself that I can run on a 10% charge for a long time. Sometimes, I even let it dwindle to the overly dangerous 1% charge, surging ahead - functioning, but barely.

Our bodies are not designed for this. Sleep is imperative. No nourishment (or the wrong kind) creates havoc. We may think one hour a week with God is enough. Mary knew otherwise, as did Helen. They knew their bodies needed spiritual fuel to keep functioning.

Twice, I have driven a vehicle that ran out of gas. The first time, I was in high school. My grandparents had given my parents their 1966 gas-guzzling Oldsmobile station wagon. While on the way to school, the car just died. I was barely able to get it pulled off the road and onto the shoulder. Thankfully, a Good Samaritan stopped and helped out. When I didn't have the proper fuel, someone else made sure I did.

The second time, I had been serving as a pastor just a couple weeks. Having completed a pastoral call, I prayed that I would make it to the nearest gas station. Instead, I ran out of gas in front of the local police officer's house. He had just filled his lawn mower. Thankfully, there was a small amount left in the gas can. I drove away, terribly embarrassed and determined not to let this happen again. My pious Martha-like mentality chastised myself for letting this happen, while simultaneously commanding myself to not let the gas gauge get below one-eighth of a tank in the future.

Why do I let my over-functioning Martha gas tank run out of gas consistently? Why do I downplay the fatigue I may be feeling when a Good Samaritan gently encourages me to schedule a little self-care? Why do I ignore all the warning signs of being low on gas, and keep willing myself to keep going, even to the point of exhaustion? When Rick says, "You need to cut back," why do I minimize the effect my overcommitment has on our marriage and my personal life?

Sometimes, I run out of gas physically. Other times, emotionally. Certainly, it happens regularly within my mental abilities. And yes, even the pastor runs out of spiritual gas when she fails to fuel her soul.

How often do we allow ourselves to be drained by an unending pile of things we "should" do with little contemplation of how much energy these tasks need? Does today's to-do list include a realistic number of items, or is it more of an overly optimistic wish list?

Are you already feeling anxious about whether or not you will accomplish enough today, this week, this month? Will you ever find enough time to finish reading this book?

How effective are we in God's kingdom when we have an overburdened spirit, taxed to the limit, and undercharged? Do we fake being content and happy because heaven forbid anyone know otherwise?

Each time I come back to Martha and Mary's story, I recommit myself to make changes. I promise to dig deeper and find out how God yearns for me to offer my best contributions to God's kingdom. My spiritual soul can't run on 10% forever. I, too, have diminishing rates of productivity and excellence of work.

Sitting in the pew during Helen's service, I yearned to have one more conversation with Helen. I wished I could go back to her house, sit at her table filled with pretty dishes and steaming cups of coffee in delicate china, and chat. I longed to explore her understanding of Martha and Mary, how she strove to balance the two tendencies. But I cannot. What I *can* do is let people like Helen and Mary inspire me to seek the life of a recovering Martha.

Unfortunately, it would be many years after Helen's service before Rick and I would have "the talk." My BFF Martha had enlisted me to be one of her best lifestyle supporters, and I happily obliged. Her "Don't quit!" mantra sang loudly in my mind. Life was full-steam ahead, despite a depleted charge and empty gas tank.

Reflection Questions:

1. Are you content with your balance between Martha and Mary? What makes it challenging for you to move in the direction you would prefer to be?

2. How would your life look and feel if you had reached the perfect harmony between Mary and Martha?

3. Like Helen, who is someone you have admired for their appropriate understanding of Mary and Martha?

Prayer:

Dear God – It's not easy to be honest with ourselves and check where we are on our spiritual journeys. Whether we have more Martha or Mary tendencies, encourage us when we struggle. Thank you for Your grace in accepting us just the way we are. May we be guided and encouraged as we walk through *The Mary Experiment*. Amen.

Part 2:

Making a Historical Story Relevant Today

CHAPTER 3

Baggage for the Journey

(Jesus said,) "Do not get any gold or silver or copper to take with you in your belts – no bag for the journey or extra shirt or sandals or a staff, for workers are worth their keep."

- Matthew 10:9-10 (NIV)

I could be called a bag lady. Everywhere I go, I haul multiple bags with me.

I overpack for every outing, prepared for any scenario. I always have a couple work options along, as well as a couple of books. Grandchild wants gum? No problem. Juice boxes and snacks for a treat at the park? Under control.

If staying overnight is involved, I have more than one clothing option. I learned this lesson the hard way. One day, Hubby Rick and I were my dad's taxi ride home from the hospital. Before he was safely tucked at home, my mom was in an ambulance on her way to the hospital. Rick went home to work, and I stayed a few extra days to assist my parents. It was supposed to be a day trip, so I only had the clothes I was wearing.

Every subsequent time I visited my parents, I brought along at least one change of clothes. And often two laptops: my personal laptop and my work laptop. You just never know.

Even a trip to the office requires multiple bags. I have my main work bag, maybe a second work bag, my purse, my lunch bag, and the bag I need to run an errand after work. Seriously. Do I really need all these bags?

Contrast this with my friend Pam. She travels a lot. For the last several years, her main residence has been overseas. She returns to the United States once or twice a year. Most of her luggage is filled with items she is delivering for someone else. On one three week trip, she had two pairs of pants, two tops and one fancy outfit to wear to a wedding. That was it!

Pam is not a bag lady.

Why am I such a bag lady? Why do I spend my life hauling things from Point A to Point B? I learned this from my mom. She couldn't leave the house with just one or two bags. She always had multiple, and more in the car.

When you are preparing for a journey, how many bags do you take with you? Do you strategically prepare for any possible situation, or do you prefer to keep things light and easy? Are you a bag person or a light traveler?

Jesus the Traveler

Jesus traveled a lot in His lifetime. It is amazing the amount of ground He covered, especially when we realize His main mode of transportation was walking. Before He was born, a very pregnant Mary made the arduous and difficult journey from Galilee to Bethlehem. After an angel made it clear that Joseph needed to move his little family away from King Herod, Joseph hid them safely away in Egypt. For the next several years, Joseph's family lived in a country with a different language, customs, clothing, and social hierarchy than they were used to. All to protect God's Son.

When it was safe, Joseph moved his family back to a little village called Nazareth in Galilee. Joseph assumed the Son of God would be safe in this remote village. Here, Jesus was raised like any other Jewish boy, with no attention drawn to who His real father was.

Annually, Jesus' family traveled from their hometown to Jerusalem for the Passover celebration. Every spring, Joseph and his family journeyed with other families from Nazareth. It was safer and easier to travel with a large group. Families meticulously planned and arranged for the multiple day trip.

One particular year, the trip was going great... until the return trek back to Nazareth. The group had traveled for a whole day without Jesus. He'd been left behind.

When Mary and Joseph discover Jesus is missing, they check the entire caravan. Nope, no one has seen 12-year-old Jesus. On the hurried trip back to Jerusalem, imagine the worry, tears, and helplessness Mary and Joseph felt. Where had Jesus been sleeping? Was He eating? What if someone abducted Him? Where should they begin looking?

It took three days of frantic searching before they found Jesus safe and sound in the temple courts. Jesus was oblivious to the angst His parents have been through. The Son of God had been hanging out and studying with the local teachers. A very casual Jesus seems mystified by His earthly parent's behavior. Surely, their first stop should have been His Father's house. Of course, He would be at the local synagogue.

We aren't provided with the emotions and feelings Mary and Joseph experienced while looking for Jesus. All they knew was that their son was missing, and they wanted to find Him. We would expect a similar reaction from a parent today when a child is missing.

Traveling Light

A seasoned traveler, Jesus made numerous trips between the Sea of Galilee and Jerusalem throughout his ministry. He traveled through the Judean Desert, land controlled by the Samaritan people - territory usually avoided by God's Chosen People. He traveled north of the Sea of Galilee to Caesarea Philippi. He traveled all around the Sea of Galilee, stopping at every little podunk village to care for fellow Jewish kin.

Can we imagine how many times Jesus noticed something strange in His travels? Repeatedly, He interrupts His travels to speak, heal, or listen to people along the route.

Jesus traveled even lighter than my friend, Pam. Likewise, He instructed the disciples to travel light. In Matthew 10:9-11, Jesus sends them into towns and villages. "Travel light," He says, "with no gold or silver or copper ... in your belts ... no bag for the journey or extra shirt or sandals or a staff."

Seriously. Not even an extra shirt? Over-packers, like me, cringe. Did Jesus forget it gets hot in the summer and people sweat? Wouldn't an extra layer during the winter keep the disciples warm when the sun dips below the horizon?

"Nope," Jesus says, "travel light. Leave the baggage behind."

Throughout the gospel accounts, Jesus and His disciples took frequent breaks during their travels. Time and time again, Jesus turned a pitstop into a teachable moment. He never missed an opportunity to enlighten others about God's kingdom.

A Life-Lesson Pit Stop

Jesus' stop in Bethany at Mary and Martha's house is such an instance. Jesus and His disciples were on their way to Jerusalem. Bethany is just a few miles from Jerusalem. This little stopover, a short break from the physical demands of foot travel, became a fortuitous teachable moment.

Sisters Martha and Mary lived with their brother, Lazarus. The family was more than mere acquaintances of Jesus. They were close personal friends, which influences how the sisters interact with Jesus. Martha feels comfortable enough with Jesus to address something stirring her heart.

Each sister has her own life journey. Their individual life "baggage" affects each sister's character and choices, how they interact with people, and what their life priorities are.

Martha is a typical bag lady, with everything necessary to ensure that she will always be a great hostess. When Jesus takes a break from His grueling travel schedule, Martha's hospitality guarantees the stop will be a respite. Guests leave with full tummies, properly refreshed and ready for the next leg of their journey. Her 'baggage' is making sure all of this happens to the very best of her ability.

Mary travels lightly. She carries just one bag, carefully packed with the most important things. The bag doesn't need to be completely filled. She relishes the empty space. For Mary, experiences are more important than possessions. Her attitude allows for flexibility and less anxiety. Quality over quantity.

While raised in the same household, siblings may view baggage differently. Why does Martha make over-packed bags her priority? Did her mother teach her how to be the most admired hostess in Bethany? Has she observed another neighborhood lady who had entertaining down to a science, who passed the hospitality mantel onto Martha?

Contrast Mary's very different baggage. Rather than stuffing every inch of her bag full, Mary loves a lighter and less cumbersome load. Most importantly, she doesn't feel guilty about this.

Life's Blueprints

Children are often the product of the environment in which they were raised. Our upbringings influence what is important to us. How and why we do certain things is colored by what we learn growing up. The situation in which you were raised is a blueprint for your life.

When a building is being constructed, a blueprint shows the size and dimensions of the building, the pitch of the roof, where the electrical and duct work will be located, the exact location of the plumbing, and a whole host of other things. Likewise, family blueprints cover a wide range of topics: how a family celebrates holidays, who is responsible for what activities, financial practices, protocol for how discipline is enforced, and a whole laundry list of other things.

The blueprint of our youth becomes the foundation of the blueprint we live as an adult. Think of how often we hear the line, "That's how I was raised." Positive and negative, these connotations are part of our blueprints. Sometimes, we use these as "good-bad" examples, determining that a negative influence will not be a part of our future life. Other times, challenging situations form so much of a family's framework that they are passed down from generation to generation.

Family traditions continue via family blueprints. My family eats oyster stew every Christmas Eve. As Hubby Rick ages, sometimes I wonder if I live with my husband or my father-in-law. When my husband comments about a behavior he observes in one of his children, sometimes I remind him that the apple often does not fall far from the tree. I only need to look at our youngest grandson, Dylan, to imagine what Rick was like as a child. It almost seems impossible that this little boy can have so many physical features and personality traits which resemble his grandfather.

This is all part of our baggage. It is part of our journey.

Baggage on Our Journey

Like Jesus, we are traveling on this journey called life. Some of us drag along lots of baggage: poor habits repeated over and over, never moving beyond a challenge, a love (or hate) for some part of our lives. Some people would like to move beyond their childhood blueprints, but have not been able to.

Others pack much lighter. Some people "will" themselves to rise above an observed behavior that irritated them as a child. Others take more drastic action, possibly even moving to a different geographical location to escape frustrating habits and routines.

While we often focus on the amount of baggage we carry, having the right kind of baggage is also imperative. Life baggage can be helpful. This is how core values are taught and caught. Teaching children to volunteer, serve others, and give of themselves is best learned by observing someone they respect model this. I admire Karl Barth's perspective when he said, "Teach the gospel daily, but only use words when necessary."

I love and respect much of what my parents instilled in me. They taught me to be hard-working, dedicated, and dependable. When Dad told me that if I worked hard enough and didn't give up, I could accomplish anything - I believed him. On good days, I still believe this is true today. This is baggage I drag along on my journey.

Like my parents, I often forget that "No" is a complete sentence. My natural inclination is to take on way too much. I struggle to make "the most important" priorities of a day the first things that I do, before anything else. I can easily be distracted by some silly thing like checking my phone, looking up one thing on the internet (which leads to 20 wasted minutes and five more sites) or making sure everything is just "so" in the house. I know these things aren't the most important baggage. Yet, often, that's what demands too much of my attention. In the moment, I forget that saying "Yes" to this baggage means I say "No" to something else.

How do we make sure we have the right baggage with us? How do we prevent ourselves from overpacking or underpacking? How can we determine when we need a break?

Too often, we focus on the baggage the world says we need: more possessions, larger bank accounts, and sizeable retirement plans. Contrarily, Jesus emphasized filling our bags with honesty, compassion, respect, kindness, and other fruits of the Spirit. It's not the tangible things that are most important, He says. It's the non-tangible.

It saddens me to watch myself and others fill our lives with the wrong things. We think a particular car or vacation, a phone, or purse, will fill an empty hole. Most often, it's a lack of contentment or peace or love that leaves us hollow. This will never be filled, even by the greatest sale imaginable.

Jesus models the importance of taking a break. He didn't get to Jerusalem as fast as possible. When His feet and soul needed a break, He refreshed them at the home of special friends. Enjoying a meal and spending time with people near and dear to His heart was a priority. Everything else on His "to-do" list waited. For Jesus, the journey was just as important as the destination.

Like Jesus, we make daily choices about our journeys. Historical blueprints from our upbringings influence our lives today. We determine how much and which parts of these blueprints we embody. Each day, we make choices. What baggage do we need for today? What baggage needs to find the garbage can? What baggage clutters our desks and brain and distracts us from what is most important? How often do we hang onto baggage because it feels like a security blanket? Do we let baggage from previous days negatively or positively influence our journey today?

Sorting Life's Baggage

After Mom died, I began going through her accumulated totes and boxes of treasures that had not been gone through for decades - more than 30 boxes and totes of things that had been moved multiple times. Hubby Rick threatened to throw the whole lot into the garbage if I did not do something about them.

I spent hours and hours going through my mom's baggage. I discovered items from my grandparents and my great-grandparents. Sometimes, I held saved items in my hand and wondered, "Why?" Yes, there were some really cool things: my Dad's dog tags from the service, my Grandfather's pocket watch from the early 1900's. Pictures from the 4-H fair where my parents met. Item after item shed light to the blueprint in which I was raised.

Some things, I easily discarded or gave to another family member. But there was a whole bunch of stuff that required more than one pass. Old pictures of ancestors whose descendants our family no longer has contact with. Funeral memorial books from generations of grandparents who had passed away. Things that were important to someone at one time.

Deciding what baggage to keep, what to get rid of, and what to pass on became a huge part of this journey. Some days, I could make decisions quickly. Other days, the process felt terribly overwhelming. I saw glimpses into my ancestors that made me laugh, others that made me cry. I saw generations of similar blueprints lived out while digging through my ancestor's treasures.

It made me evaluate what historical things I personally value and want to keep... and what needs to hit the garbage can. What are the most important treasures from my life journey? What is more trivial? What baggage am I comfortable with someone else potentially going through? What is important enough to keep?

Each time a box was emptied, I felt lighter and a sense of accomplishment. The process became a metaphor for my life. I questioned other areas of my life that I needed to sort through and eliminate. Often, this baggage weighs me down and prevents me from focusing on the most important aspects of life.

Traveling Companions

Having the right companions with us on the journey is also key. Jesus didn't travel alone. Neither should we. He surrounded himself with a small group that supported Him daily. He modeled for us the importance of sharing the responsibility with others. Too often, Martha's choose to do it alone rather than shoring up a supportive network.

Jesus fully embraced His life journey. The blueprint of His early years influenced His ministry years. He knew when to drop negative baggage along the side of the road and not let it drag Him down. He made sure He had the right traveling companions. He packed the right kind of baggage and left the rest behind.

As I try to be influenced by Jesus, I am discovering the freedom of packing lighter in this journey of life. Will I ever stop being a bag lady? Probably not. Yet, I challenge myself to be more aware of the invisible baggage I drag with me. I want to make sure that Jesus is the most important traveling companion in my daily life.

Reflection Questions:

1. Do you relate to the metaphor of over-packing or under-packing? Who is someone you know that packs the opposite of you?

2. Reflect upon the blueprint of your life. What aspects of your childhood blueprint greatly influence your life today? What pieces of this blueprint are baggage you've tried to leave along the side of the road? What pieces do you carry that you need to leave behind?

3. When do you normally take a break in your life journey? What does this break look like? After a break, how do you feel?

Prayer:

O God - In our day-to-day lives, it becomes easy not to see the bigger journey of life. Help us embrace our individual journeys. Bring travel companions into our lives who enhance our journey and encourage us to travel closely with You. Remind us of the most important baggage to bring along and what pieces of baggage we can leave behind. Amen.

CHAPTER 4

It's Your Name

"Look! You will conceive and give birth to a son, and you will name him Jesus."

- Luke 1:31 (CEB)

I've had my personal identity compromised twice. My name, the most important way to identify myself and the words that made me unique from everyone else, was snatched away from me.

My identity was first jeopardized when a person, representing themselves as me, contacted the church treasurer from one of the churches I was serving as the pastor. The e-mail requested that almost $20,000 be wire transferred to an out-of-state account. Unfortunately, the church volunteer thought the email really *was* from me and followed through with the request.

Initially, I was so caught up in trying to get the money returned to the church that I didn't comprehend how my personal identity had been exploited. When I understood this, I tried to walk the precarious balance beam of honoring the church's best interests as well as protecting my own identity. I found it challenging to distinguish between being "Pastor Dianne" and simply "Dianne." The two were intertwined as I tried to uphold and protect the church's name and reputation, as well as my own.

A couple weeks later, Hubby Rick and I were chaperoning teenagers on a youth mission trip. One day, our work site was a transitional living location. We parked our vehicles on site. Throughout the day, we were in and out of the cars, getting tools and water. Sometime during the day, my bag was stolen from inside the car. Nearly every piece of my personal identification disappeared: my driver's license, bank and credit cards, personal and business keys, and a variety of other personal items. Once again, my identity was vulnerable.

In life, there are very few things that we can truly call our own. Our name is one of them. Parents carefully chose a child's name. Sometimes, it is selected because of the name's particular meaning. Possibly a child is named after someone the parents felt inspired by or because of familial roots.

When a person hijacks your name, it is very unsettling. Although I have sat with people as they shared stories how their or an acquaintance's identity was stolen, it is different when you are the one in the hot seat. Out of all the potential pastors in the United States, why did an email target me as a victim? Did the person who helped themselves to my wallet want every piece of my personal identification, or just the cash? If the person only wanted the money, why did they take the entire wallet?

After my identity had been stolen twice, I felt like my name was no longer mine. As I tried to externally downplay the situation, internally, I felt violated. Cheated. Hacked. My life is so plain, boring, and vanilla. Being Dianne Deaton Vielhuber isn't very glamorous. Yet, the one thing that is all my own, my name, felt marred.

Choosing a Name

People quiz expecting parents about what they are going to name their child. Some parents address their unborn child by the intended name. Other parents wait until their child is born before selecting just the right name.

Even when a birth name is given, sometimes, nicknames arises. This maybe a person's choice ... or not. My husband's birth name is Richard. I can tell what stage of life someone became acquainted with Rick based on how they address him. Childhood friends call him Ricky, a name he detests. His high school buddies call him Rich. After high school, people called him Rick.

Even with a different nickname, Hubby Rick is the same person with the same personality and sense of humor. Whether he signs his name, "Rick" or "Richard," he is a beloved child of God, unique and deeply loved by God.

Because names are distinctive, a particular name can cast positive or negative feelings. Parents avoid a name because they previously knew a person with this name, and it doesn't elicit warm and fuzzy feelings. Think of the family name at the school where you attended, the one that everyone knew was a troubled family. We can just as easily recall the family name everyone admired.

It appears that Martha, Mary, and Lazarus have a respected family name. When Lazarus dies, "many Jews" grieved with the sisters. I am confident Martha's parents carefully chose their daughter's name. In first century Jewish culture, women held very little status. Their name was the one way they could separate themselves from other Jewish women. It was one of their only sources of identity.

First century Jewish people most often spoke Aramaic, the language Jesus conversed in on a daily basis. In Aramaic, the word "Martha," means "the lady," the feminine form of the masculine word "master." The root word of Martha has secondary meanings of "bless, strengthen, and command." In its Hebrew form, "Martha" means "bitter." For Jewish people, the concept of "bitter" not only relates to grief, but also to strength.[1]

Based on her name's background, should it be any surprise that Martha was the welcoming committee

---

[1] Abarim Publications' Biblical Name Vault: Martha, *www.abarim-publications.com/Meaning/Martha.html#.XHGjduhKg2w*, (October 1, 2019)

when Jesus arrived? Jewish people expected this lady to be strong-willed, in charge, and wanting to bless others with her hospitality. We see Martha living out the name she was given... and doing a splendid job of it! Martha embraced her given name. She embodied it.

For those of us with personality traits similar to Martha, we might ask, "What's wrong with that?" We applaud her take-charge nature, her no-nonsense approach to serving others, and her ability to whip up a meal, drinks, and a comfortable atmosphere with seemingly little effort. This is what we expect of a woman named Martha.

Martha is not the only name associated with a particular personality. Some names are so well understood, they do not need an introduction:

Mother Teresa

Martin Luther King, Jr.

Leonardo da Vinci

Walt Disney

Rosa Parks

Michael Jordan

When we hear these and other notable names, we automatically create an image or picture of who this person is, what they stood for, and their contributions to society.

Now, look at this list of names:

Adolf Hitler

Jeffrey Dahmer

Osama Bin Laden

Lee Harvey Oswald

Satan

We garner few warm fuzzies from this list. Clearly, we are influenced by names and the association.

The Names "Jesus" and "Mary"

Jesus is another name that needs no further identification.

The name "Jesus" carries with it all kinds of baggage. What image or picture comes to mind when you hear the name Jesus? Is it one of a man who performed a whole bunch of really cool miracles? Or is it a picture of the man who hung on a cross and died? Is your image one of a baby squealing in a manger, or one of a man walking on water? Is the name "Jesus" difficult for you to understand, impossible for you to wrap your head around?

The name "Jesus" was specifically chosen for the Son of God. Gabriel tells Mary, Jesus' mother, what to name her baby. Joseph, Jesus' earthly father, was also told by an angel to name Mary's baby Jesus.

Why "Jesus?"

Jesus derives from a Hebrew word that means "savior." The title Christ, also attributed to Jesus, means "messiah" or "anointed" in Hebrew. "Christ" indicates that Jesus was commissioned by God for a special task.[2] His name becomes the very foundation of his heritage, existence, and purpose. Jesus Christ is anointed by God to be the Messiah that saves the people of the world. It's a name that deeply identifies his role with humanity.

Probably the most common female name in the New Testament is Mary, the name of Jesus' mother. How ironic is it that Martha's sister has the same name as Jesus' mother? The name "Mary" may have been based on a similar Egyptian name, which means "my beloved." In its Hebrew form, Mary derives from the name Miriam, the sister of Moses. While the Hebrew meaning is not known for certain, possible meanings include "wished for child," or "sea of bitterness," or "rebelliousness."[3]

In the New Testament, Mary was a more popular name than Martha. It is very easy to confuse the various Mary's in the Gospels. Who was Mary Magdalene? Do we know for sure if she is the woman who wiped Jesus' feet with some very expensive perfume? Can we keep straight the various Mary's who

---

[2] Paul J. Achtemeier, *The HarperCollins Bible Dictionary*, Revised Edition (San Francisco: Harper 1996), 150.
[3] Behind the Name, *http://www.behindthename.com/name/mary*, (October 1, 2019)

arrived at the empty tomb the Sunday after Jesus' crucifixion?

While there are many different Mary's who followed Jesus, only one Martha is named. She has a strong name, one she seemingly feels obligated to fulfill. With "strength" and "master" as part of the underlying meanings of her name, she is a "doer" who tries to keep everyone else on task as well.

I wonder if Martha ever felt a bit jealous of Mary and her ability to just "be." Was there a sliver of Martha who yearned to slow down and not be in charge all the time? Does Mary have the same opinion of Martha that we do? Or was her opinion of Martha quite different from what we read back in the story? If this same Martha lived today, would she have liked for someone to change her view of herself, so that she would not have to be the New Testament's version of a busy-body that never stops?

Baptized in the Name of Jesus

As a pastor, I have been gifted the wonderful opportunity to be involved in the baptizing of many people: infants, youth, teens, and adults. Every time I am a part of creating this special covenant with God, I am humbled. Before the person is baptized, I add a few drops of water from the Jordan River to the baptismal water - water from the same river where John the Baptist baptized Jesus. It is a symbolic way to connect the two baptisms. Pouring water over the person's head, I say, "*(Person's name)*, I baptize you in the name of the Father, and of the Son, and of the Holy Spirit. Amen."

For me, baptism is a holy moment. A child of the Almighty is named. This person is surrounded by the three persons of God and becomes a member of God's holy family. No matter what happens to this person, their name is etched in covenant with the Holy One. Even if their identity is compromised, or they change their name, this person will always be a beloved child of the One who created, redeemed, and sustains them.

After Jesus was baptized, the Spirit of God broke through the heavens and said, "This is my Son, my Beloved, with whom I am well pleased." (Matthew 3:17)

Pause for just a minute. Place your hand on top of your head. Say these words aloud to yourself, "This is my child, my Beloved, with whom I am well pleased."

Before a baptism, I choose a special bible verse for that person. I pray the verse will be a sentence of encouragement throughout that person's faith journey. When a mom shared with me that her grown daughter makes sure her baptismal bible verse is part of the décor in every place she lives, my heart swelled. This young woman wants to be inspired by her special bible verse daily. Thanks be to God!

Baptism happens within the context of a faith community. Traditional baptism liturgy charges the church to be a part of the raising up of this person throughout their faith journey. Spiritual development does not happen in a vacuum. It happens best when others surround this person with prayers, encouragement, and support.

Your name is special to more than just you. Your name is important to God. You are God's beloved child. No matter what you have or have not done, God is well pleased with you. With Martha. With Mary. In God, your identity can never be snatched away or compromised. In God, you and your name are enough.

Reflection Questions:

1. Has your personal identity ever been compromised? If so, what were the circumstances? How did you feel about your name and identity as you navigated through that situation?

2. What is the story behind why your parents chose your name? If you are married and you changed your name, is there a way that you kept your maiden name as a part of your identity?

3. If you do not know the meaning of your name, look it up. Are parts of the historical meaning of your name part of your personality? Do you struggle with living up to the meaning of your name?

4. When you think of yourself as a beloved child of God, how does this make you feel? What words would you use to define your relationship with God?

Prayer:

Holy God - In our throw-away society, we often get rid of things quickly. I pray that we see our name as one of the few things that has meaning and importance, as it was chosen just for us. May we truly know and feel that we are beloved children of Your family. Amen.

Chapter 5

Welcome, Jesus!

Instead, they should show hospitality, love what is good, and be reasonable, ethical, godly, and self-controlled.

- Titus 1:8 (CEB)

His official title was Ring Sheriff. And he had the badge to prove it.

Most people would have called three-year-old Miles the Ring Bearer. At this wedding, however, Miles graduated into the role of official Ring Sheriff. During the wedding rehearsal, Miles proudly showed me his badge. He held it tightly in his hand, letting me see the badge, but not wanting to relinquish it. Before the wedding, I inquired if his badge was ready to rock-and-roll. "Yep," was the answer I received, as Miles turned to show his badge proudly clipped onto the lapel of his miniature black tuxedo.

There may have never been a prouder three-year-old than Miles. He took his job as the official Ring Sheriff very, very seriously. Miles strutted around the wedding celebration with the badge visible to all.

Deep down, aren't we a little like Miles? Don't we want a badge that officially designates us as someone special? Maybe it's for a role we have, or recognition of our best gifts and graces. The things that we proudly proclaim as something we put our heart and soul into. Wouldn't we love even one picture of us wearing the badge, that we could plaster all over our social media accounts?

Whether these badges are visible or invisible, we hang onto them just as tightly as Miles did. What badge would you like pinned to the lapel of your jacket? Maybe it's a badge of being a good listener. Or the badge of being on-time. The badge of being an outstanding parent or spouse. We like to slap invisible badges on our coats, our bags, and our self-awarded sashes. Whether anyone else can see them or not, we wear them proudly. Sometimes, we may even remind people of these self-awarded badges.

Our friend Martha wore a badge proudly: the best hostess in Bethany.

The Great Hospitality Experience

When Jesus and his buddies showed up at Martha's house, advance notice or not, Martha never skipped a beat. It was a significant honor to have this special man enter her house. Jesus healed people, restored their sight, and calmed terribly rough waters at the Sea of Galilee. Martha challenged herself to make this meal one her guests would never forget.

Warmly welcomed guests reclined around a low table, surrounded by comfortable cushions and pillows. While the servants washed the guest's feet, Martha picked vases of fresh flowers and artistically displayed them on the table. She selected the best wine from her pantry and made sure there were no water spots on the wine glasses. A quick plate of olives, grapes, apricots, and nuts were beautifully arranged on platters and offered as appetizers, along with chunks of still-warm bread and rich olive oil. Guests grazed on these tasty treats while Martha finished roasting the lamb, perfectly seasoned with fresh herbs snipped from her garden.

Martha seemingly pulls off this dinner party with nary a hitch. Never mind her stove is an open fire or that the water is drawn from the city well, several blocks away. Jewish law required that meat and dairy could not be prepared in the same area. Going between the two kitchens – one dairy and one meat – would have increased preparation time and made washing dishes more laborious.

With her hospitality badge proudly pinned to her robe, Martha seemingly keeps up with the details of hosting a dinner party. Internally, however, she's LOSING IT! With so many details, she simply does not have time to be with her guests. She's managing the meal prep, making sure the wine carafes are full, and constantly refreshing the appetizer trays. It's exhausting to handle everything by herself.

Except, she *could* have help. Sister Mary is available. Even though she may not be on Martha's level, there are some things Mary could do. She must be aware that Martha could use an extra set of hands.

I love to host parties. I privately covet Martha's hospitality badge and would love to have one plastered to my outfit. Whether a visit is planned or not, I pride myself in being ready for guests. I can quickly throw together a meal. The dining room table is picture-perfect ready.

Often around Christmas, Hubby Rick and I host a Christmas Open House. I go all out, with beautiful decorations and homemade food. I challenge myself to make everything perfect, from the softly glowing candles to the chairs strategically positioned to maximize seating capacity. The night before, the serving tables are tastefully decorated and the serving bowls positioned, with little name tags next to them indicating what will fill them the next day.

No matter how prepared I am or how late I stay up making sure everything is just right, the last hour before the party evaporates. Arranging the food and making sure everything is in its place takes time. Hot drinks must be hot and cold ones, cold. I am doing 10 things at once. Rick watches football, hopefully showered and shaved. It's 10 minutes before the party begins. He is oblivious to what is going on in the kitchen. The doorbell rings. The first guests have arrived. Early...

My hands are full of veggie trays, cute bowls of dip, and baskets of crackers. Rick is still putting on his shoes and belt. Like Martha, I want to run to Jesus and say, "Can You PLEASE tell him to help me? I'm exhausted, and the party hasn't even started."

Yes, even Martha has a limit. Not wanting her hospitality badge to be tarnished, she lowers herself to admit that a little help would be wonderful. She approaches Jesus, puts her hands on her hips, and makes her case for Jesus to instruct Mary to help her.

Just expressing her tightly held feelings is a relief. Unfortunately, the aura of pleasure lasts only momentarily.

Jesus looks deeply in Martha's eyes and says, "Martha, Martha ..."

Anytime Jesus says the same name two times in a row, take note. His response may not be what we want to hear, but it WILL be what we NEED to hear.

While Martha doesn't say the words, I think that I know how she feels. I imagine the words swirling around her mind, "But Jesus, I'm doing this all for You!"

So often, this is where our right intentions go wrong. We think we are doing something for someone else. But who are we kidding? If we are brutally honest, there is a place deep down inside of us that knows, most often, we do some things not for someone else... but for ourselves. We wear the badge of service, while truthfully just wanting everyone to admire our dedication, commitment, and skill. We want to earn the badge of being a great person, an excellent leader, an outstanding friend or spouse. We hold tightly onto all the reasons why we should be awarded a particular badge because, well, we *deserve* it.

I tell people that we host these Christmas Open Houses because it is my Christmas gift to our friends and the folks from the faith communities that I have served. Truthfully? There is a place inside of me that yearns for people to reaffirm how beautifully decorated the house is. I long to impress people with my cooking skills. I want people to be amazed that I can lead worship and preach on Sunday morning AND host a Christmas party within a couple hours of the last worship service. I yearn for people to award me a badge because people feel extremely welcomed in our cozy home.

I am no different than Martha. My motives and desired outcomes are very similar. I chase a badge of recognition from other people to justify my over-stuffed, over-fluffed, and over-scheduled life.

A Biblical View of Hospitality

Webster's defines "hospitality" as the friendly reception and treatment of guests or strangers, or the quality or disposition of receiving and treating guests and strangers in a warm, friendly, generous way.

In the Bible, hospitality often focuses on how people responded to strangers and aliens - people unlike themselves. The Old and New Testaments place special emphasis on caring for widows, orphans, and the poor. This is why Ruth harvested food for herself and her mother-in-law, Naomi. Boaz made sure his workers kept grain in certain areas for destitute people.

With few hotels and restaurants, biblical travelers depended upon complete strangers for lodging and food. Because Bethany was so close to Jerusalem, it may have been more comfortable for Jesus and his buddies to stay at Martha's house than find lodging in Jerusalem. Since Martha's an expert on rolling out the "Welcome, Jesus!" mat, stopping at Martha's house may have been a regular part of their journey to Jerusalem.

Think about a memorable hospitality experience. How did you feel when the red carpet was rolled out for you? What made this example one that brings back fond memories and warms your heart? Most likely, it's not because the carrot cake was beautifully displayed on a gorgeous cake stand. Or because the soup was out of this world. We remember great hospitality because the host made us feel included. They took time and interest in our lives, no matter how many other guests milled around the room. We left feeling special and loved.

This is the type of hospitality the Almighty yearns for us to experience within God's family; for us to extend and to receive. Hospitality is rooted in the very nature of the Trinity. The three persons of God - Father, Son, and Holy Spirit - form a perfect union of hospitality, in which each person compliments, supports, and encourages the others. Badges aren't necessary, because there is constant mutual love and respect between the three persons of the Trinity. They fully complement each other. Within the Trinity, we find expressions of both Mary and Martha.

Unfortunately, some of us may have experienced less than holy encounters of Christian hospitality. Whether this happened within the context of a church, individually with a person who proclaims Christian faith, or within a small group of people, poor hospitality can be devastating for the receiver. As sinful human beings, our experience of extending perfect Christian hospitality falls short. Our red carpets become stained and worn. Our happy endings turn into disappointed guests. Our crafted menu is barely eaten.

What is often the root behind disappointing hospitality experiences? Often, we say that we are doing something in the name of Christ or for the glory of Jesus, when we're truthfully doing it for our own benefit. We want the badge slapped on our chest. We yearn for recognition of all the good things we do. We long for someone to tell us that, "You're the best."

When this happens, Jesus' words to Martha are words we must hear, "Martha, Martha ... Mary has chosen what is better, and it will not be taken away from her."

Moving away from a 100% Martha-like existence means stripping away the badges we love to attach to our lives. It means shifting the yearnings of our heart from wanting the badge for ourselves to becoming part of the Trinity's team. It challenges us to understand hospitality as something not for our benefit, but for the guests and strangers we encounter every day.

Before we give up these badges, we might be a little like the Ring Sheriff. During the wedding ceremony, Sheriff Miles stood next to the groom. He tugged at the groom's coat. He wanted the groom to hold his hand, not the bride's hand. As the service progressed, Miles became antsy and found it hard to stand still. After the rings had been removed from his silky pillow, and his job was officially over, he threw the pillow into the aisle. He was *done* being the Ring Sheriff.

Moving towards a Trinitarian-based understanding of hospitality takes time. We may make progress and think we have mastered not needing a badge. But then, we get frustrated and throw in our "pillow." We want those relinquished badges back. We want recognition, accolades, and "atta boys."

It's so hard to let go of being Martha.

It's even harder to hear Jesus say, "Martha, Martha ..."

We forget that Jesus has already rolled out the red carpet for us. Jesus has accomplished everything necessary for our eternal life. We cannot earn this gift, try as we might.

When Jesus says your name, He encourages you to demonstrate hospitality. Love what is good. Be reasonable, ethical, godly, and self-controlled. These badges are stored in a safe place. God has them waiting for us.

Reflection Questions:

1. What are the badges that you would love to have plastered on your chest? Why did you choose these?

2. Recall an exceptional example of hospitality you have experienced. Remember one that was not so great. What made the great experience outstanding? Why did you feel uncomfortable in the not-so-great situation?

3. The Trinity is one of the tenets of the Christian faith that people may find difficult to understand. How does the concept of perfect hospitality within the Trinity resonate with you?

4. Write the words from Titus 1:8 on a card: *Instead, they should show hospitality, love what is good, and be reasonable, ethical, godly, and self-controlled.* Carry this card with you until you have the words memorized and written onto your heart.

Prayer:

Almighty God - Thank you for a wonderful example of extreme hospitality within the Trinity. While we know that we cannot replicate this example perfectly, may we discover where our heart lies. Allow us to move towards serving Jesus with our lives rather than serving ourselves. May the badge of being Yours be enough for us. Amen.

CHAPTER 6

When Sitting is Oh, So Hard!

When they didn't find Jesus, they returned to Jerusalem to look for Him. After three days, they found Him in the temple. He was sitting among the teachers, listening to them and putting questions to them. Everyone who heard Him was amazed by His understanding and His answers.

- Luke 2:45-47 (CEB)

For over two weeks, my life revolved around sitting. Huddled in a chair, I tried to get comfortable next to my mom's bed as she journeyed through the last days of her life.

The irony was not lost on me. Here was this woman who had spent nearly all of her life *doing*. With a front-row seat, my sisters and I repeated many of her same traits: grasping opportunities to do what we could for someone else; lacking an ability to say "No;" and challenging ourselves to do and do.

But in her last days? Mom simply was *being*.

The doing had come to a screeching halt. Her body was wearing out. No longer able to move or care for herself, she was now totally reliant on others.

My sisters and I spent hours sitting next to her bed. Early on, we fed her, just as she once did for us. When she could no longer swallow, we rinsed the inside of her mouth with little pink sponges provided by Hospice. For years, Mom 'washed other's feet' in how she cared for others. Now it was our turn to "wash" hers. We massaged lotion onto her hands and feet, and carefully covered her lips with Carmex. We read *The Upper Room* to her, a daily devotion book she had followed for decades. Sometimes, we just listened to her favorite hymns. And we prayed. Over and over, we prayed the Lord's Prayer. We told her good-bye. We celebrated communion together. We did things we thought would make her last days meaningful.

More than once, we quickly convened like chicks gathered around the Mother Hen, thinking these were the last moments of her life. As we sat by her and waited, we watched this woman, who had spent her lifetime doing, simply *being* before she received her final reward.

Was our mom teaching us one final lesson? Could we accept that sometimes, it's OK to just sit and be? We knew the joke was on us, her daughters. She had raised three daughters known more for their Martha-ness than for their Mary-ness. Yet, here we were, held captive by one more life lesson Mom taught us in the last days of her life.

Could we learn to just sit and be?

Sitting at Rabbi Jesus' Feet

We can easily turn Jesus' visit to Mary and Martha's house into a moral lesson about which sister is doing the "right" action and which sister is missing the boat. If this is all we allow this story to be, then we miss the depth of understanding that longs to be uncovered.

This story is more than simply comparing Martha, who is "doing," and Mary, who is "being." This story is about two women whom Jesus uses to teach a radical lesson. One sister welcomes Jesus into her house. The other sister is taught by Jesus, something extremely unexpected in Jesus' day.

Martha fulfills the very traditional Jewish woman role of offering excellent hospitality. As a Jewish woman, Martha basically had two obligatory purposes: be a wife and a mother. Since it seems that Martha is unmarried, she takes the responsibility of being a homemaker seriously. Meanwhile, Mary sits at Jesus' feet.

The Jewish understanding of "sitting at someone's feet" is different from ours. It's not kids sitting with the pastor during a children's message. It's not grandchildren gathered around a grandparent as a special story is shared. It's not a student listening as a teacher reads a storybook.

First century Jews sat at someone's feet for the purpose of formal and higher education. The sitting person is instructed by someone and learns something. It's a master instructing a pupil. It's a sage sharing with an apprentice. It's a philosopher imparting wisdom to valued students.

This is what 12-year-old Jesus did while at the Temple during the Passover. Jesus sits with the teachers, the rabbis, in the temple courts. He listens, asks them questions, and discovers their interpretation of Jewish law. Already, the student impresses the teachers with His understanding and explanations.

A rabbi is a teacher of Judaism. Rabbis *needed* followers. A first century Jewish man could not be a rabbi without disciples. As rabbis discussed God's word, students or disciples would literally "sit at his feet" and be trained as a disciple of that particular rabbi. Students asked questions and became part of the teaching exercise.

Throughout the gospels, Jesus is identified as a rabbi. The Pharisee Nicodemus acknowledges Jesus as a teacher or master, when he says to Him, "Rabbi, we know that You are a teacher who has come from God."

In Mary and Martha's traditional Jewish household, their world revolved around caring for their home and family. Neither their mothers, grandmothers, nor they themselves were included in studying the Torah. There was no reason for a woman to sit at a rabbi's feet. A first century Jewish woman's role was exactly what Martha was doing.

At Martha and Mary's house, Jesus employs the traditional style of teaching. It just so happens that Mary, a woman, participates in this rabbinic teaching circle. When Jesus responds to Martha, he isn't condemning Martha for fulfilling her traditional woman's role as much as he's commending Mary for becoming one of the students who sits as his feet and learns. Mary has purposefully chosen to drink in Jesus' knowledge. She is enthralled with the question and discussion learning style. She wants to learn how to live out God's commands from Rabbi Jesus.

When Mary takes the posture of being a learner, she wordlessly states her clear desire to be a disciple of Jesus. As she listens to the dialogue between Jesus and the other disciples, her knowledge and understanding of God becomes very personal. Mary does not want this information second-hand. She wants it directly from Jesus the Rabbi. She puts herself at His feet, ready to have her knowledge and understanding challenged and expanded.

By allowing Mary to sit at his feet, Jesus also makes it very clear that a woman's value goes beyond what she does. Jesus acknowledges that a woman's role goes beyond bearing children and tending to the house. Jesus indicates that a woman's status is not defined through a relationship with a man. Jesus redefines a woman's most important role. He makes it clear: it is her relationship with God. Jesus does not only allow a woman to sit as His feet; He encourages it.

As 21st century people reading back into an event that happened 2,000 years ago, it's nearly impossible to fully understand the depth and implications of Jesus' actions. When Mary sat at Jesus' feet, a woman became part of the conversation. She had the same opportunity to explore what it means to be a disciple of Jesus, and in turn, God. When Jesus said, "Martha, Martha ..." He wasn't focusing on rebuking Martha for performing the normal perfunctory responsibilities of a Jewish woman. Instead, He was saying, "Martha, Martha. There is more than cooking, cleaning, and hosting when you are a part of God's kingdom. Please, let's discover this together."

Can Martha look beyond traditional Jewish roles and see that being a disciple of Jesus means a new radical way of life for her?

A New Definition of Discipleship

Radical moves are not usually encouraged, suggested, or applauded. While not afraid of change, there are times I have advocated a more moderate approach in the hope of less fall-out, reduced dissention, and fewer messes to clean up afterwards.

This is not how Jesus rolled. His lessons were bold, extensive, and profound. While he was often encouraged to make less dramatic moves, Jesus chose to clarify God's kingdom with drastic, rigorous, and sweeping new interpretations.

Rather than living by the letter of Jewish law and following all 613 traditional Jewish commandments,

Jesus tells His disciples to whole-heartedly follow two commandments: love God and love your neighbor. Not one to forgo the opportunity to help a person in need, Jesus purposefully healed on the Sabbath. Instead of accepting a ho-hum commitment to God as enough, Jesus asked the rich young ruler to give *all* of his life to God, including his vast financial assets.

Whether with a group of students at his feet, walking through Samaria, or riding in a boat on the Sea of Galilee, Jesus' teachings were counterintuitive to what Jewish people had practiced for years. His words, actions, and encouragement were nothing short of radical.

So radical, they got Him killed.

How radical was Jesus' gospel? Listen to His words:

> *"For all those who exalt themselves will be humbled, and those who humble themselves will be exalted." - Luke 14:11 (NIV)*
>
> *"And whoever does not carry their cross and follow me cannot be my disciple." - Luke 14:27 (NIV)*
>
> *"In the same way, those of you who do not give up everything you cannot be my disciples." - Luke 14:33 (NIV)*

Jesus casts a whole new vision of discipleship within God's kingdom. His priorities are different from what other rabbis taught. Jesus says it's what's on the inside of a person that becomes the hallmark of discipleship. When a person's heart, mind, soul, and strength are fully turned towards God, what they do on the outside represents what they believe and feel on the inside. When a person accepts this radical vision introduced by Jesus, they find something worth dying for.

This vision completely enamored Mary. She was so caught up in what Jesus taught that pouring wine seems silly. Making sure the bread tastes heavenly wasn't important. Mary was drawn into Jesus' radical vision for God's kingdom: hook, line, and sinker.

Mary made discipleship personal. Lingering near Jesus' feet, she knew the best way to develop a relationship was spending time with the person. Unfortunately, Martha thought serving Jesus was more important than listening to Him. She was still trying to minister to people through their stomachs.

I look at Mary and blush. For so many years, I have gotten it wrong. I thought discipleship was about more doing and being active. As a pastor, too often I focused on running the church and my Christian life as a business, wanting to get more and more accomplished. Success, as defined by the culture around us, became more important than spiritual growth. Too often, I chose not to look at Rabbi Jesus and ask, "How might I really learn to love You and my neighbors?

Can I ever discover the art of sitting at a person's feet? Can I come to grips that sometimes "good enough" is

OK? Will I allow the pull of perfectionism to not override my desire to know Jesus as a personal Savior and friend?

One Last Life Lesson

As I sat with Mom in her last days, I often reflected upon how just a couple weeks earlier, I had taken a bold step. When I voluntarily stepped away from serving two churches as their pastor, some people were disappointed. Others were confused. I knew my decision could lead to pastoral ministry career suicide.

The timing was not lost on me. Had I still been serving as a pastor, I would not have had the flexibility to spend all those hours sitting next to Mom's bed. I would have tried to juggle and keep various balls in the air, Martha-style. Instead, many aspects of my life were temporarily put on hold so I could simply be with my mom. How crazy is it for my sisters, Mom, and I, all Martha-driven women, to be spending hours on end together, doing very little? For most of these hours, my mom wasn't able to communicate. Yet, my sisters and I kept vigil, rarely leaving her alone.

There was one last lesson Mom wanted to share with us. Could we discover the art of sitting? Being? Listening? Praying?

In the weeks after Mom's passing, I reflected upon this life lesson. Would I continue to run my life at 90 miles an hour, or could I slow down and learn to sit? Honestly, the transition took time. I would discover the joy of being less committed, only to find myself again taking on things without any contemplation or soul-searching. I had spent so much of my life saying "Yes" that learning to say "No" did not come easily.

Could I stop the need to justify saying, "No"? Could I find joy and purpose in simply sitting at Rabbi Jesus' feet, if only metaphorically?

Holding Class with Jesus

Whether we physically sit at Jesus' feet or not, we choose what life lessons we take away from this story. Even today, Jesus holds class regularly. Do we envision sitting with Rabbi Jesus, soaking in all the wisdom and direction offered to us? Like Mary, can we forgo the hubbub of the kitchen and make it a priority to sit at the Master's feet? We choose whether to invest in a relationship with Rabbi Jesus. Will we have the easy (and the difficult) conversations with the One who we sometimes feel disappoints us?

The first woman to receive a degree from Oxford was renowned English crime writer and poet Dorothy Sayers. Dorothy explained why she became a devoted follower of Jesus this way:

> *I think I have never heard a sermon preached on the story of Martha and Mary that did not attempt, somehow, to explain away its text. Mary's, of course was the better part – the Lord said so, and we must not precisely contradict him. But ... Martha was doing a really feminine job, whereas Mary was just*

> *behaving like any other disciple, male or female; and that is a hard pill to swallow.*
>
> *Perhaps it is no wonder that the women were first at the Cradle and last at the Cross. They had never known a man like this Man – there never has been such another. A prophet and teacher who never nagged at them, never flattered or coaxed or patronized; who never made arch jokes about them; who never treated them either as 'The woman, God help us!' or "The ladies, God bless them!"' who rebuked without [demeaning] and praised without condescension; who took their questions and arguments seriously; who never mapped out their sphere for them, never urged them to be feminine or jeered at them for being female; who had no axe to grind and no uneasy male dignity to defend.*[4]

Yes, both Martha and Mary have lessons to teach us and skills to impart upon us. I hope to hear Jesus say, "Dianne, Dianne. There is more than cooking, cleaning, and hosting when you are a part of God's kingdom. Please, let's discover this together."

---

[4] Dorothy Sayers, *Are Women Human? Penetration, Sensible, and Witty Essays on the Role of Women in Society* (Grand Rapids: Eerdmans, 2005) 68.

Reflection Questions:

1. Have you had the opportunity to simply sit with someone for an extended period of time? How comfortable was this for you? Was there something you discovered about yourself during this time?

2. How do you define radical? What radical move(s) have you made in your life?

3. What parts of Jesus' message are most difficult for you to embrace?

4. What does the word "discipleship" mean to you? Do 21st century Christians embrace discipleship in the way Christ taught?

5. Do you have a place where it is easier for you to simply be? Why this place? If you don't have such a place, how might you create a place where you can be?

Prayer:

Rabbi Jesus – It may be difficult for us to accept and understand the complete radical nature of the gospel You shared. Thank you for accepting everyone into Your teaching circle. Help us to keep this circle as wide and diverse as You established. Create deep within our hearts the desire to learn to simply sit at Your feet and be with You. Amen.

CHAPTER 7

Busy, Busy, Busy

But Jesus often withdrew to lonely places and prayed.

- Luke 5:16 (NIV)

It should have been just a normal phone call. When I asked the person on the other end of the line how their day was, the person replied, "I am just so busy. Busy, busy, busy."

Millions of Americans say these words EVERY. SINGLE. DAY. I am no exception. When the person shared with me how busy they were. I thought to myself, "I'm not sure you are any busier than I am!" Really, Dianne? How do YOU know how busy someone is?

After this little incident, I try to refrain from using "busy" when someone asks how I am. In fact, I have developed a significant dislike for the word "busy." I think we should insist on an indefinite moratorium on the sentence, "I am just so busy."

What is "busy?" As old-fashioned as this may be, I pulled the *Oxford Advanced Learner's Dictionary* off my bookshelf and looked it up. *Oxford* gives four meanings for "busy:"

1. having much to do: "Doctors are busy people," or occupied with something: "She's busy with her homework."

2. full of activity: "a busy street."

3. being used: "a busy telephone."

4. too full of detail: "The wallpaper is too busy for the bedroom."

Let's focus on definition number one, which says we have too much to do or are occupied with something. Nothing in the definition reveals whether the action is 1) necessary; 2) important; or 3) going to change the world or someone's life. There is no distinction as to whether the action is a good choice, a mediocre choice, or a poor choice.

For some Americans, "busy" is a stamp we proudly wear. We WANT everyone to know that our lives are tumbling full of activity. Some people cannot imagine life without an overflowing schedule. Not being busy might indicate that a person isn't important enough, has no friends, or isn't wanted or needed. Often parents wonder, "Will my kids be left behind if they aren't scheduled seven days a week?"

In other parts of the world, the "busy" badge is frowned upon. These cultures think Americans are simply crazy. Imagine living in a society that promotes afternoon siestas and leisurely eating meals. A full month of summer holiday. Americans say, "How I long to live in a place like this..." Yet we continue our helter-skelter, overly busy ways and make choices where these behaviors are impossible.

A few weeks after I had stepped back from serving two churches as the pastor to pursue writing, my friend Lisa called. She congratulated me on this decision and asked what I planned to write about. I shared with her my hopes for this very book. Lisa admitted that she is a Mary and how her ultimate Martha-like husband can be overwhelming at times. We commiserated how my husband is more like her, and I am more like her husband.

Then, Lisa shared how sometimes she dislikes attending certain events, knowing there will be people present who will lament about how "busy" they are. Her honest words resonated with me: "We can all be busy. What some people forget is that we all choose to be busy. I choose not to be so busy, and I don't want to be put down because I have made this choice."

Can I get an "Amen!" for my sister, Lisa?

Martha is described with these words: busy, preoccupied, worried, distracted, pulled away by all she had to do. Martha made the conscientious decision to be these things. No one imposed these feelings upon her. She made the choice. Martha could have skirted by with yesterday's leftovers and day-old bread. She chose not to.

Likewise, we make many, many choices every day about how engaged we will be. We all have lots of things happening in our lives: family, work, finances, maintaining a household, volunteering, and being a never-ending taxi driver hauling kids from one commitment to the next. We feel it is absolutely necessary to appear we have it "all together" every day of the week, every hour of the day. Our calendars are overstuffed, we eat too many meals in our vehicles, and we rely on texting rather than face-to-face interaction, even for the most important relationships in our lives.

How do we usually feel at the end of the day? Stressed, tired, exhausted, and trying to figure out how we will do it all over again tomorrow. And the next day. And the next...

Do you ever have a fleeting moment where you just want to stop and watch the beautiful horizon colors change as the sun slips away? Do you yearn for a snow day where the kids can simply play outside with no agenda other than coming inside for hot chocolate topped with marshmallows? We dream of a day away, with nothing to do but whatever we want... yet that day is the one thing we never schedule.

How Big is Your Garden?

On our Wisconsin farm, we grew a large garden. During my childhood, gardening was less about being in vogue and all about feeding a family as economically as possible.

Our garden had mounds and mounds of potato plants. Long rows of beans, peas and carrots. A strawberry patch next to a hedge of raspberry bushes. We cut fresh, regrown lettuce all summer. Tomato plants bore big, ripe, and juicy produce that became tomato juice, spaghetti sauce, and whole canned tomatoes. We depended upon wheelbarrows full of watermelons, cantaloupe, cucumbers, and squash. Onions and corn and gooseberries were regular garden attendees.

The bane of any garden? Weeds. While we used techniques such as mulching and roto tilling, keeping up with weeds was a never-ending job. Every spring, I vowed not to let the weeds become bigger than the plants. But as the summer wore on, weeding slipped down the priority list. After all, weeds wouldn't feed us throughout the winter. We focused on harvesting and preserving instead.

For many Martha's, our life-gardens are bigger than we can handle. Weeds crop into life and distract from the bigger and more important aspects of daily life, until our gardens feel out of control. Focusing on "harvesting" the important produce of life is often overshadowed by weeds that consume too much attention.

Why do we let our life gardens grow beyond boundaries that we can manage? Why does busyness consume us? Why don't we ask for help? What are the consequences of being so busy tending to our own garden that we miss out on something that would fill our lives with joy?

Productive people often set high expectations for themselves. Rather than seeing what they have accomplished, they focus on what didn't get done. The urgent demands too much of our attention. Focusing on surviving today, we never take time to let our dreams evolve and become realities.

Fear of disappointing someone often leads to over-commitment. We chase the momentary satisfaction of looking good in the eyes of another and allow shallow internal feelings of ourselves to be just fine. When asked to take on an additional project, we struggle to say "No," even when our gardens are filled with weeds.

There are a variety of reasons why Martha's let their gardens get too big:

- We think some new technology will help us "save time," when often it just becomes something more to manage or an additional distraction.
- We want control of the project and don't trust someone else.
- We wait until the eleventh hour, when it is no longer feasible to ask for assistance.
- We have this crazy desire to feel needed.
- We are passionate about too many things.
- We don't want to let others down.

I am sure you can add more ideas to this list.

Most Martha's have big gardens full of great things. While we may be growing lots of meaningful things, being over busy is not always what is best for us, our relationship with God, or God's kingdom. We need time to rejuvenate and dream. Creative ideas seldom flow when they are sandwiched between one demanding task after another.

When 'Busy' Slides into Sinful Behavior

It is difficult to look at our lives and see that our busyness is usually not a scheduling problem - It's a heart issue.

In the Gospels, I am struck by how often Jesus took time away from His ministry to just be with God. Repeatedly, we see times that Jesus got up early in the morning and prayed. Before many big life events, Jesus prioritized quiet time with God.

Ernest Hemmingway once said, "Most people never listen." As much as we would like to believe that we listen, I know there are many times when I thought I was listening... and I wasn't. Too often, I chose not to prioritize time to listen at Jesus' feet. When we fail to follow Christ's example and listen to God, we miss great opportunities God wants to place in our lives, but we never hear about.

My call to pastoral ministry happened when I was in my 30's. Two people were extremely clear with me about the direction that my life should go... and I didn't listen. One day, when I felt God speak to me directly, I realized this was the real deal. God was calling me into pastoral ministry.

Later, I wondered how many times God had tried to communicate something, but I was so busy being a Martha that I missed it. It's hard for overly busy people to be attentive with God. When we focus so much energy into what we think we should be doing, we become bleary-eyed and dull to God's presence in our lives. We lose the ability to hear God speak into our hearts.

Prioritizing work and productivity comes at an enormous cost. When we tend a garden larger than we can manage, we lose the awe of God's kingdom. When fulfilling a to-do list becomes our main priority, we no longer are fulfilled by God. It becomes easy to seek approval from the world and culture, rather than discerning God's ways for our lives and our little part in God's kingdom.

Psychiatrist Carl Jung said, "Hurry is not OF the devil. Hurry IS the devil." At the height of my Martha-like behavior, I did not grasp that overcommitment could be sin. By continuing to advocate and promote a life garden that was way beyond what I could manage, weeds were sprouting all over. Too often, I looked for instant validation and approval. I forgot that I could not point people towards Jesus if I also needed their approval. More deeply, it saddened my heart to see myself not living a life that I encouraged others to seek. When members and friends of the churches I served did not want to bother me with something because I was "so busy," something had to change.

Successful people have discovered this secret: they get more done when they have taken the time to slow down and fill their souls. Success should not be measured by outward accomplishments and accolades. As I challenged my definition of success, I realized it actually is a mindset. The process began with clearly identifying what is most important to me.

The Five Most Important Things in my Life:

What is most important to you? If you had to limit your life to simply the most important things, what would you choose? Let's go through a little exercise to help you determine what are the most important veggies or fruits in your life garden.

On the lines below, identify the five most important things in your life - the things with the highest priority. Don't think too deeply about this. Usually, the most important things are what initially comes to mind.

1. ______________________________

2. ______________________________

3. ______________________________

4. ______________________________

5. ______________________________

As often happens in life's journey, something unexpected comes along. You can no longer support all five items on your list. Look at your list and cross off one thing. What remains are the four most important things in your life.

After a brief period of things going well, a pothole comes in your life. This pothole is more challenging than the last blip. Because of this, you must now give up something else on your list. Cross off one more thing, leaving the three most important things in your life.

Unfortunately, bad things do happen to good people. This time, it is not just a pothole. It's a devastating valley. It's life changing. It's painful. You keep living, but now, you must eliminate one more item from your list. What remains are the two most important things in your world.

Just when you thought life could not get any worse, it does. You are now required to give up one of the last two remaining items. I know this seems unrealistic and completely unfair. However, cross off one more item from your list.

Look long and hard at the one item still on your list. This is the single most important thing in your world. Nothing has higher priority. Push comes to shove, this is the last thing you would be willing to give up in your life.

Now, pull out your calendar or where you keep track of what you do on a daily, weekly, monthly, and annual basis. Evaluate how much time you spend on the five things you listed. Approximately, what percentage of your time do you spend on these most valued areas of your life? Take particular note of how much time you spend on the single most important item of your life.

Next, pull out your checkbook(s), bank statement(s) or where you track finances. Evaluate what percentage of available resources you contribute to these most valuable players (MVP's) of your life. Where does the single most important aspect of your life fall on your resourcing list?

As you look back over your calendar and finances, if the top five items on your list are not the highest priorities for your time and resources, what is? List all the ways you spend time and resources not on your MVP list. How close are the two lists? Compare the two lists: your initial MVP list and where you actually spend your time and resources. Many of these things are important. These are good things. Yet, should these items take a higher priority than your MVP list? Why or why not?

This exercise may seem dramatic. Sometimes we need memorable exercises to help us clearly evaluate our lives. Actually, we find a biblical example of this happening in the Old Testament story of Job. A highly successful man, Job had a great family, wealth, and no cares in the world. God is so sure of Job's devotion, Satan is granted permission to test Job with stipulation: he can't lay a finger on Job himself. God is confident that Job will endure this test - Job won't give up on his faith.

Job loses absolutely everything: his animals and source of income, his children, and his home. In the midst of all these troubles, Job says, "The Lord gave, and the Lord has taken away; may the name of the Lord be praised." Every time I read this story, Job's unshakable faith humbles me. Even after four of Job's closest friends try to convince him to forsake God, Job stays true in his faith. Yes, he would like to know why this has happened. But his faith in God never wavers.

Every time I take a group of people through this listing exercise, I put myself through the ropes as well. In doing so, I realize there are some MVP's that I say are important, yet receive very little time, energy, and resources. I am always shocked and dismayed by how many things on my "busy" list are simply busyness.

Recovering Martha's will not be able to make dramatic changes to how they spend their time, energy, and resources overnight. While we can will ourselves to do this, every time I try this approach, it works until about noon the next day. Some unexpected event happens, and suddenly, I am rearranging my schedule. This new item is not bad or unimportant, but I struggle with letting the seemingly urgent take over.

Each time a new opportunity comes along, think of how these fit into your self-identified MVP list. Lots of opportunities are worthwhile and noteworthy. However, that doesn't mean they line up with your most valued areas. Adjust your MVP list over time, as priorities change at different life stages. Choosing to invest into something outside of the MVP list will pull time, energy, and resources from chosen MVP's.

We can be more alive than we realize, if only we would just let our facades down and embrace our MVP's as truly the most important aspects of our lives. Stop looking for external affirmation and allow ourselves to feel rewarded from the inside first.

When we find time to listen to God, we hear how to devote our "best" resources towards our top five MVP's. Every choice we make has an opportunity cost. Every choice we say "yes" to means we say "no" to something else. In reflecting upon all the years and years that I allowed too much busyness in my life, I think of all the potential MVP opportunities that I missed. I missed listening to God when great opportunities were placed before me. If I had only listened.

Job longed for God to speak to him and share why the awful testing happened to him. Eventually, God dramatically spoke to Job. After God's long discourse, Job humbly admitted to God and his friends, "Surely I spoke of things I did not understand, things too wonderful for me to know." Job gifts us a great reminder: Questioning the "Why" something happens is not nearly as important as remembering the "Who" will journey with us throughout life.

A More Helpful Response

We ask each other, "How are you?" because this is what good manners has taught us to do. I often wonder: do others really want to know how I am? Or do they just want to know what activity has been consuming my life?

As we respond, we mentally check-off the unfinished jobs waiting for us, or remember the long list of unanswered emails clambering for a reply. We think of the unpaid bills or piles of laundry. We prefer to plan a vacation, but question if there is money to do so.

Rather than simply wanting to hear about each other's to-do lists, can we seek each other's hearts? Rather than asking, "How are you?" maybe a more helpful question is, "How is your soul?" or "How is your heart today?"

It may not be very comfortable to ask these questions, unless the person is part of your inner circle. An alternative word for "Busy" may be "Blessed." Or "Grateful." Or "Thankful." Shifting your perspective is an important step in shifting your priorities.

We will never really examine the darker corners of our lives unless we pause our lives and allow ourselves to listen to God.

Celebrate the Small Victories

It will take a few more years for this recovering Martha to find the right sized garden. It's two steps forward and one step back... over and over and over.

These days, I try to look at the daily choices that I make and evaluate them more on effectiveness than efficiency.

It was a beautiful Saturday summer day filled with promises of blue skies and 82 degrees. Hubby Rick coaxed me into the car, along with a cooler and some tie-down straps. Kayaks were on sale. We purchased two and took them on their maiden voyage on one of Rick's favorite local lakes. My only decision was what color kayak I wanted.

Yes, I could have spent this time knocking an item or three off my to-do list. But Rick is one of my MVP's. My relationship with my husband is a high priority. One way I prioritized this relationship was doing something Rick chose. We had a great time paddling around the calm lake. The landscape surrounding the lake reflected off the pristine water. It was a lovely afternoon.

Rather than trying to achieve a perfect life, let's put our time, energy, and resources into having a meaningful life. We can be so busy that we don't have time to live. Let's choose life over busyness. Can we adjust the size of our life gardens so they are more manageable? Will you let your list of personal MVP's guide your choices? Will you intentionally develop a personal relationship with God, center it around listening, and allow it to undergird your very being?

Reflection Questions:

1. When someone asks you, "How are you?" what is your most common response? How does this fit into your view of busyness?

2. What weeds are in your life that distract you from what is most important?

3. What do you feel are the reasons why you are often too busy? What internally keeps you saying "Yes" when you could choose to say "No?"

4. How did going through the exercise of selecting your five MVP's make you feel? What did you discover about yourself?

5. Do you feel that you listen for God? Why or why not?

6. Name a small victory where you recently made a life-giving choice.

Prayer:

Lord God – Forgive me for too often living a hectic, harried, and overly busy life. Place in my heart the desire to live a meaningful life that focuses on what I hear from You. Help me look deeply into my heart and clearly identify my MVP's. May this list include a life filled by You and with You. Help me listen without judgement when someone shares their frantic life. Place in my heart the gift of empathy to just be a person who can listen. May I find satisfaction in life with You and work daily towards a less frantic life. Amen.

CHAPTER 8

Feeling Let Down

But those who think themselves great shall be disappointed and humbled, and those who humble themselves shall be exalted.

- Matthew 23:12 (TLB)

She was disappointed in me, and she was making sure that I knew it.

My siblings and I agreed it was time to move our mom from a two-story house into an apartment. When the ideal apartment became available, we quickly moved forward with plans. We had repeatedly discussed this plan with Mom. At one point, she begrudgingly agreed. But now, she had a different opinion.

It was moving day. The rented truck was in the driveway. Additional family would be arriving soon to assist. The utilities had been switched. We were ready to make the move.

Everyone, that is, but Mom...

Not ready to relinquish control, our Martha-like mom decided to have "the talk" with my sister Denise and me before anything went into the truck. She was not happy with the decision. She was disappointed that we felt she needed to move. The talk led to an awkward and uncomfortable start of moving day.

Let Down by Those We Love the Most

As disappointed as my mom was with me, imagine Martha's disappointment with her sister. Martha spent years and years alongside Mary. As young Jewish girls, they would have discovered early-on how to assist with household responsibilities. I imagine them hoeing the garden together, kneading bread dough daily, taking turns churning milk into butter, and washing guest's feet when they arrived at their house.

Mary was fully aware of Martha's Type A personality. Mary may have previously received criticism when she had not lived up to Martha's expectations. Rather than trying to motivate Mary again, this time, Martha appeals directly to Jesus. I imagine Martha stewing in the kitchen, rehearsing the words she will use. Martha convinces herself that Mary will not be able to turn down Jesus' request to assist her.

If Martha felt let down by Mary's lack of assistance, imagine Martha's initial reaction when Jesus *affirms* Mary's decision to sit at His feet. Jesus' response is not what Martha envisioned or anticipated. As disappointed as Martha feels towards her sister, her disappointment towards Jesus may have been even stronger. Martha discovered that those we love and admire the most also have the greatest potential of disappointing us.

"Those Who You Value the Most Will Disappoint You the Most"

Shortly after I started seminary, I began serving two rural congregations as a student pastor. Student (i.e. rookie) pastors are paired with a seasoned minister with more experience to help them navigate the steep learning curve of serving as a clergy.

The churches I served were geographically very close to where I called home. It made sense for the person who had been my pastor for several years to become my mentor. We knew each other well, and had previously worked together in ministry.

About a year into serving these churches, Hubby Rick and I became engaged. We did not ask my mentoring pastor to preside at the wedding. It's an understatement to say he was disappointed. One day, he shared with me how he felt. During this conversation he said, "Dianne, there will come a time when those you value the most will disappoint you the most. Today, this has happened to me."

Once again, I did not have a solution to resolve this situation. I explained why we asked someone else to preside at our wedding, but nothing I said seemed to ease the disappointment he felt. I had let him down terribly.

Sticky Situations and Tricky Relationships

In every meaningful relationship, there will be a point when one of the parties in the relationship feels let down and disappointed.

- A spouse feels their partner is more committed to their job than to their marriage.
- A child feels their parents' rules are much stricter than the rules of their friends' parents.
- Your boss belittles you for taking significantly longer on a project than they budgeted for.
- An elderly parent gives a material possession to another loved one, when it was promised to you, and you feel you "earned" this item.
- You are going through a tough time. None of your close friends extend the extra support you need.
- Your life is falling apart. You are disconnected from the church. No congregational members and friends call and see what's going on.

Identify a relationship in which you felt someone let you down - not just a little, but a lot. Rethink how this situation arose and played out. Did the person know how upset you felt? Was the hurt addressed? Were your feelings ever reconciled?

From Martha's perspective in this story, a question arises: is it possible for faith-filled people to move beyond sticky situations and tricky relationships? Can we permit ourselves to feel disappointment and hurt without judgement? It is not easy to honor personal feelings and still validate another person's position.

When a person feels hurt and disappointed, they often just want the other person to acknowledge their feelings and emotions. Sometimes, the "person who hurt" may not be aware how deeply disappointed the "has been hurt" person feels. While not easy, it is usually best for the "has been hurt" person to let the "person who hurt" know how they feel. This is usually uncomfortable. However, unidentified and unacknowledged disappointment usually leads to bitterness. Carrying around hurt feelings seldom allows for resolution.

How can faith-filled people address their feelings towards someone who has let them down, when the "person who hurt" knows this happened and seemingly chooses not to do anything about it? Very carefully. These situations require lots of diplomacy, listening and careful wording. The "has been hurt" person wants acknowledgement and recognition of their feelings. They want the "person who hurt" to admit their fault and hear their side of the story. Sometimes this is possible; sometimes it is not.

What about the times when you've listened and heard the other person... and neither of you were able to move on? Is resolution possible? There are times when one party can move forward and the other person lacks closure. When we find ourselves lacking closure, how do we forgive and let go of our hurt feelings?

My normal response is to try and "earn" back a person's trust and respect. I go out of my way, compensating for actions the other party interpreted as "poor behavior." Sometimes, additional effort is recognized and appreciated. But all too often, it only makes the resolution mountain higher and more impossible to scale.

With a Martha-type personality, it is difficult for me to let go of soured relationships. Often, I try and try and try... and nothing seems to help. Occasionally, time will soften the disagreement, and people can re-establish a relationship. Other times, it seems absolutely impossible to ever move beyond the hurt and disappointment.

Jesus' Example of Dealing with Sticky Situations

Let's see how Jesus dealt with Martha. When Martha came to Jesus, He listened. He didn't dumb-down her feelings or emotions. He took time to hear and affirm her point of view.

Jesus also dealt with the situation immediately. He didn't let it brew and morph into something beyond the current situation. Martha wanted a response... and she received one - even if it wasn't the response she anticipated or expected.

Notice how Jesus says, "Martha, Martha, you are worried and distracted by many things. One thing is important. Mary has chosen the better part. It won't be taken away from her." As Jesus repeats Martha's name, he gently exposes her hidden armor and engages her on a more personal level. Jesus acknowledges and describes Martha's feelings. He doesn't try to brush her feelings under the rug. He deals with them directly and without hesitation.

I often wonder how Mary felt as Martha and Jesus have this conversation. Is she quietly cheering Jesus on for addressing this perpetual issue with Martha? Does she feel Martha received the "talking to" she deserved, but didn't have the courage to address with her? Is Mary embarrassed for Martha and taken aback by her forthrightness?

It seems Mary does not want to involve herself in this sticky situation. Instead, she quietly watches from the sidelines.

Feelings and Forgiveness

Forgiveness is tricky, because we are dealing with real people's feelings. There is no simple forgiveness recipe. Each situation requires unique and tailored interactions and responses.

The Apostle Paul did give us a model for forgiveness:

> *Get rid of all bitterness, rage and anger, brawling and slander, along with every form of malice. Be kind and compassionate to one another, forgiving each other, just as in Christ God forgave you.*

- Ephesians 4:31-32 (NIV)

Forgiveness can be long-term and obtainable when we root it in the forgiveness God extends to us through Christ Jesus. Forgiveness without God's grace at the core won't last. This forgiveness is temporary and short-lived. Long-term and sustaining forgiveness acknowledges our own need for forgiveness - just as other people also need forgiveness. We need forgiveness no less nor any more than the next person. When we aren't fully able to forgive someone else, often we still struggle with fully accepting God's forgiveness for ourselves.

I am not a forgiveness expert. Rather, I'm the person who has a great deal of experience in trying to understand my need to receive and extend forgiveness. I have made more mistakes in this area than I care to admit. Yet, this does not mean I give up on forgiveness.

When I am the person who feels that I have been hurt, and I desire repentance from another person, I often address this situation directly. It's a great day when the person acknowledges my feelings and apologizes. Numerous times, the other person was unclear of how I felt. They were unsure how to deal with the situation. They are notably relieved when I privately and gently address it.

When I have been the person who did the hurting, again, I also try and address it directly. The result is often a mixed bag. Some people are ready to move forward and try and create a safe spot. Others want something from me that I may or may not be able to extend. We cannot go back and undo a situation. My role is not to take on someone else's feelings. I am responsible only for my own feelings, what I say, and how I react. My personal experience also says once I have addressed something, it's time to let it go. Rarely is it helpful to revisit the same person and situation a second, or third, or fourth time. Each time a situation is rehashed, people's feelings get stirred up. Any healing that might have happened will likely need to occur again. Rarely is there progress with repeated attempts for peace.

When is it appropriate to involve another person? In Matthew 18:15-17, Jesus encourages us to deal with the problem initially with just the two people. He does say if the other person does not listen, take someone with you for the benefit of having a witness. Personally, I only like to include another person when I feel this person has additional information that may be helpful or is acting as a mediator.

Today, social media makes hurt, disappointment, and forgiveness much trickier. People have more opportunities to say things with less accountability. If you have underaged children who use social media, be mindful how these tools can have positive and negative effects.

Is it appropriate to attempt to resolve a long-standing situation? Yes, if both parties are ready to address it with the understanding that forgiveness must be rooted in God's forgiveness of all.

For conflict avoiders, these suggestions will be met with anxiety and trepidation. These concepts may be completely outside of your comfort zone. Yet, I find Jesus' response to Martha prescriptive in how we can handle sticky relationships and situations.

Seldom is forgiveness something that you put on a to-do list and cross it off, once and for all. Because feelings are such an integral part of forgiveness, it tends to be one of those things where we hope we make progress over time.

Overcoming sticky situations is difficult whether you tend to be more Martha- or more Mary-like in your approach. Even without a record of Martha and Mary's response to Jesus' words, we know that the sisters keep a strong relationship with each other. When their brother Lazarus dies in John's gospel, both sisters are not afraid to question Jesus' behavior. They appear as an unhappy united front and question why it took so long for Jesus to come to their brother's aid.

Moving Beyond Sticky Situations

On the day of Hubby Rick's and my wedding, the mentoring pastor was not involved in the ceremony. He continued as my mentor. Did we ever quite reach the level of trust that we had previously? Probably not. Could we still support and encourage each other and continue a professional relationship? Absolutely. This only came about because we made a conscious choice and effort to make it happen.

As far as my mom's disappointment in moving to the apartment? It was difficult for her to accept a new living situation. As we chatted about the benefits of her new home, she slowly let go of her disappointment and accepted her current reality.

One day while speaking to a crowd and his disciples, Jesus says, "But those who think themselves great shall be disappointed and humbled, and those who humble themselves shall be exalted." So often, we are disappointed after we think too highly of ourselves. We seem to feel we are owed something. When we elevate ourselves and our attitudes, we put ourselves in a position of letting others down. It will happen - it's just a matter of when.

Martha wanted everyone to know how hard she was working. She was so caught up in earning a badge, she missed the opportunity to exalt herself in Jesus' and Mary's eyes by remaining humble.

Did Martha feel more let down by Mary's inaction or Jesus' reaction? We aren't privy to this information. Does it matter? What we do know is that Martha had the opportunity to learn a humbling and significant lesson from Jesus. While we were not present at the dinner party, we have the same opportunity. Sticky situations and tricky relationships can be great opportunities for us to shift perspective, challenge us to see a larger picture of reality, and develop trust in God. This begins when we move beyond the disappointment of being let down and allow for the Holy Spirit to surprise us with an outcome beyond our imagination.

Reflection Questions:

1. Go back to a time you felt let down and disappointed. What in your behavior might have contributed to this situation becoming an issue?

2. When you have let someone else down, what is your natural response? Do you try to "earn" their trust back? Do you quickly move on? Do you avoid dealing with the situation? Are you able to move on and keep a relationship with this person or not?

3. Identify a situation where you or someone else was let down, and there was a surprising and amazing end to the story.

Prayer:

Almighty God – Too often, we try to exalt ourselves rather than deferring this role to You. We forget Jesus' encouragement to remain humble. Help us forgive those who have hurt and wronged us. If there is someone from whom we need to ask forgiveness because we hurt them, place this name on our hearts. As we speak with them, give us an open heart to hear their hurt and acknowledge their feelings. Amen.

CHAPTER 9

The Unexpected Response

You see, at just the right time, when we were still powerless, Christ died for the ungodly.

- Romans 5:6 (NIV)

We ask a question knowing what we want the answer to be.

Or make a statement expecting affirmation... only it doesn't come.

This is what happens to Martha.

"Tell her to help me," Martha says to Jesus. While different translations use various words, most versions choose to use the word, "Tell."

In Martha's world, she's already taking a *huge* step by enlisting Jesus' help. For most type-A personalities, asking for help is not easy. We find it much easier to assist other people than to make ourselves vulnerable and request assistance. Martha's willingness to ask for help is, well, simply remarkable.

Her request takes an interesting path. Martha deflects potential disappointment by not going to Mary. Instead, she drafts Jesus to be the heavy hitter. Internally, Martha has already determined that Mary won't be able to turn down Jesus' request.

Everything was going so well... until the unexpected response.

Like Martha, I have gone into millions of conversations anticipating the potential outcome. I know what I want to say and the ideal response that will be elicited because of the interaction. I will walk away a happy camper. I have already convinced myself that there is only one possible outcome.

Not so fast, Martha/Dianne. Things do not always turn out the way we plan. We watch Martha come face-to-face with the lesson that just because we think something is important does NOT mean everyone else agrees with our assessment. Our agenda may not be everyone else's agenda. Our request may not be what someone else desires.

"Tell her to help me," Martha says.

She has already formulated Jesus' answer in her mind. She anticipates the words Jesus will say. The "I know I'm right" cheeky grin is already creeping onto Martha's face as she anticipates Jesus' words. Her chest is filling with pride because she knows best. The whole conversation should take about 10 seconds, tops.

Except Jesus' response is completely different from what Martha expected. With compassion and a soft expression on his face, his heart knows she will be caught off-guard by his response. His words could turn her against him.

Yet, carefully... tactfully... he goes ahead with the surprise comeback.

"You are worried and distracted by many things. One thing is necessary. Mary has chosen the better part. It won't be taken away from her."

Only Jesus can look into Martha's soul and know what Martha wants is not what she needs. What Martha wants is not what Jesus wants. Jesus yearns for her to stop her busyness and sit for a while. Take a load off. Just be with Him.

When does Martha realize that Jesus' response will not be her expected response? What happens to the grin and the "I know I'm right" stance she has taken? What expression now fills her face?

Oh, how I wish those details were included. But they aren't.

Instead, the story ends with Jesus' heart-felt and deeply meaningful words. The author of Luke's gospel only wants us to focus on Jesus' unexpected response and nothing else. His words are enough.

Worried and Distracted

Post college, I began attending a church in the mid-sized community where I lived and worked. I became acquainted with many couples who were similar in age to my parents. For some reason, I gravitated towards them and developed special relationships with a few of them.

One such couple was Howard and Rhoda. Physically, Howard's slight frame and bald head reminded me of my dad. His personality only added to the semblance. Like me, Rhoda loves music.

For the last 15 years of Howard's life, Rhoda spent nearly every waking moment worrying about her husband. Well, truthfully, Rhoda worried about *everything*. When her husband was diagnosed with Parkinson's, her worry only escalated. Was he taking the right medication? The right dosage? How would the disease change him physically and mentally? What should she be doing now to prepare for the future? Was she giving him the best care possible?

With compromised health, Howard was moved to a nursing home. After three months at this care facility, Howard returned home. Rhoda pulled together a list of CNAs who provided Howard daily care. The calendar quickly filled up with covered shifts, and an open-door policy was established at their house.

Slowly, Howard's health changed. Adjustments were made. Choices about quality over quantity of life were prioritized. Every day, Rhoda wondered if she was doing enough to care for her ailing husband.

The time came for Howard to go on Hospice. In the last days of Howard's life, Rhoda questioned if she had done enough. What more could she have done? Distracted by her emotions, Rhoda vacillated between feeling like she should do more or quietly let him slip away. A self-proclaimed worrywart and Martha, one day, I suggested that her most important role was to sit by Howard's bed and simply hold his hand. The tears rolled and emotions trembled as Rhoda tried to understand that worry would not add any value or minutes to Howard's life.

Personally, I find worry as one of the least helpful of emotions. We can convince ourselves that something will or will not happen, purely through worry. Worry can suck the life and energy right out of people, making their ability to see reality more difficult. Jesus declared worry as unnecessary, when He shared the Sermon on the Mount. "Can worry make you live longer?" - Matthew 6:27 (CEV)

Throughout His ministry, Jesus coached lots of people to avoid worry: the synagogue leader Jairus, whose daughter was dying; the disciples as they watched Jesus walk on water; while teaching on the mount and on the plain; and as He spoke of the end times. Jesus assured all who would listen that worrying will not add a single day to their life. Let things take care of themselves, He encouraged.

Jesus also encouraged Martha to quit worrying. "It's distracting you from what is important," He tells her. Like Rhoda, many Martha's create needless worry by thinking they haven't done enough. Most often, Jesus says, it's not that the Martha's of the world have done too little. It's that they have allowed their doing to replace an opportunity to sit at Jesus' feet and discover the peace He offers us.

When we only look for what we could or should have done, we completely miss the peace waiting to quiet our hearts and souls. Whether worry is promoting us to action or it's the unstoppable busyness spinning in our heads, it often distracts us from focusing on what really is most important in the moment. When worry becomes a defining value, we overlook the more pressing opportunity. We miss seeing the forest through the trees as we put energy into "could haves," rather than honoring the moment at hand.

One Thing is Necessary

As full and crazy and distracting as life can be, Jesus summarizes His response in four words. "One thing is necessary."

My cell phone rang at 8:55 AM on a Sunday morning. I was scheduled to play piano at a church for worship. I assumed worship was at 10 AM. Everyone else knew the time had changed to the church's summer worship schedule of 9 AM... except me. Worship began, and I arrived as soon as I could.

After worship, we chatted about the miscommunication. I encouraged everyone to keep perspective. Worship happened, just with one less hymn. In the grand scheme of things, how important was this mistake? On a scale of 1 to 10, with 10 being a catastrophic event and 1 being barely a blimp on the map, where did this fall?

For me, this barely registered as a 1. Three days earlier, Howard had passed away. Five days previous, dairy farmer friends from Kansas had lost their entire dairy operation in a tornado. Many animals were just... gone. Remaining animals were recovering and had been relocated to other dairy operations. In the days since the horrific storm, Rob, Lisa, their family, and hundreds of friends focused on restoring water and electricity, along with salvaging what little was left. Yes, worshipping God is SO. VERY. IMPORTANT. But a little miscommunication about worship time? Nothing compared to what Rhoda and our dairy farm friends were experiencing. At the time, it felt silly to contemplate this incident as anything other than an unfortunate little error.

What is the one necessary thing that Jesus yearns for us to know? What should we be most concerned about and consistent with in our living?

A personal relationship with the entire Trinity God. A relationship that is built on investing time, energy, and effort into knowing God in a deeply personal way. A relationship that is individual, sustaining, and consistent. A relationship that is growing, nurtured, and prioritized over everything else in our lives.

Knowing God is more important than possessions and assets. It's more valuable than any tangible item I can hold in my hand. It's so much of my very being that, without it, I would not be who I am.

When I go through the exercise in Chapter 7, crossing off things from what is truly most important, the final remaining item is always my personal relationship with God. This is more valuable to me than Hubby Rick, his children, and our six grandchildren. It's what I would choose over work, good health, and our beautiful home. It's the last thing in the world that I would give up.

This is what Mary focuses on in her life. It's what Jesus wants so desperately for Martha to choose as the very core of her being. Jesus longs for Martha to desire this over a hospitality badge, fresh baked bread, and the best wine in the cellar. Likewise, Jesus yearns for you and me to feel a deep desire in our lives to want to be sustained and upheld by this relationship, which Jesus based on unconditional love and acceptance.

When we choose this as our one necessary thing, we admit that we do not have everything about this relationship figured out. Yes, there are many, *many* aspects of God that confuse and bewilder us. Some days, we will be upset and angry with God. While we may sometimes want to walk away from God, we don't completely turn our backs on God, because we know there is something life-giving in this relationship.

Our one most important thing is what sustains us when horrific storms blow into our lives, leaving it in shambles. A relationship with God allows us to have a wide range of emotions with God, from love and peace, to anger, disappointment, and hurt. As we develop a life-giving relationship with Christ, we see that this relationship is always available to us - even when others have disappointed us and failed in our eyes.

People often share with me that they gave up on God when they felt that God gave up on them. I don't think God ever gives up on us. God simply shows up in different ways from what we expect:

- God shows up in a casserole delivered when a storm ravages our lives.
- God shows up as an offer to help that arrives at just the right time with the necessary pieces of equipment.
- God shows up with a hug that holds tightly until tears subside.
- God shows up as a texted prayer that hits all the right notes for the day.
- God shows up as a trailer and driver, ready to move the remaining cattle to a safe location.

And so many other countless ways.

Search your memory. When did someone or something just show up in your life completely unannounced that made a difference in your day? Maybe, just maybe, that was God reaching out to you in a creative and meaningful way.

As much as God shows up in our lives, are we as committed and consistent in showing up with God? Do we begin and end our days with prayer? Do we find a verse of scripture on which we can hang today's activities so we can keep the right perspective? Do we set down our phones, tablets, and technology instruments long enough to make sure God gets a little of our attention, too?

When we take the story of Martha and Mary seriously, we identify what the one necessary thing in our lives is. You made your choice when you completed the exercise in Chapter 7. Revisit this choice. Confirm this is what you feel is the most necessary item in your life.

Mary's Choice Is Always Her Choice

Jesus closes His response to Martha with these words, "Mary has chosen the better part. It won't be taken away from her."

Before we assume that Mary has "won," let's see exactly what Jesus says.

I feel Jesus purely prefers Mary's choice. He doesn't say that Martha's choice is wrong; He just shows preference for Mary's choice and assures Mary that her choice will not be taken away from her.

Life is full of choices. We choose our occupation, where we live, what we drive, what we wear. With so many choices and opportunities in our lives, often we find ourselves with more than one "great" option.

Sorting through to discover the "best" option takes time and effort.

If we fail to choose God's preference at this time, does this mean we won't ever arrive at the place God would love for us to be? Absolutely not. I feel God doesn't preordain only certain choices to reach specific results. I believe we take a very active and involved role in paving our life path. Sometimes certain choices may affect the route we take. God can help steer potential opportunities back into our lives if we choose.

Jesus simply reminds Martha that she has made a choice. While Martha can accomplish more during one of her bad days than most people do all week, her whirlwind of activity, energy, and accomplishment comes with a price tag. Too often, she chooses the urgent and immediate over what will sustain her for the long-haul. Immediate success can be a blessing and a curse. The "here and now" can overshadow sustainability for the future. When we put so much energy into surviving the day, we lack the energy to look beyond the immediate and see where God may be calling us.

Jesus encourages Martha to extend Mary grace for her different choice. In a world that often wants us to do more, Jesus whispers, "Be still and know that I am God." Rather than trying to prove our love for someone by what we do, Jesus appreciates that Mary has chosen to let her time and attention mean something. She wants to enlist Christ's help in becoming the best version of the person God created her to be.

And this will never be taken from her.

In His quiet and humble way, Jesus takes Martha's situation and de-escalates it to a more manageable issue. He encourages Martha to focus less on something that is of this world and shift her perspective towards something that will give her energy and life, rather than simply drain her. Jesus appreciates how sitting at the feet of God instills hope, passion, and love into a person - versus accomplishing a laundry list of to-do items that leave us exhausted and beat.

Making Our Choice

As I sat with Rhoda during Howard's last days, we often talked about choices. The choices she had made earlier in terms of Howard's care. The choices she was making that very day to keep him comfortable and at peace. After years of being able to manage Howard's care on a day-by-day basis, in these last days, Rhoda could no longer make choices about how and when Howard would leave this world. All she could do was wait.

It was terribly humbling for Rhoda to relinquish control over something she'd held onto so tightly for so long. While choices about medication and such were made, in the end, the timeline was not something anyone other than Howard and God could control.

Howard passed very peacefully on Ascension Day. Three busy Martha's were down the hall in the kitchen, chatting away and busily doing. Mary-like Howard took his last breath quietly and unassumingly. "Ms. Martha" Rhoda immediately felt guilty for not being by his side at that moment. Maybe she wasn't physically in the room, but Rhoda had 'been there' for years and years and years. Howard's quiet faith, sustained for decades by a personal relationship with God, was all that was necessary in the end. And it was not taken from him.

Reflection Questions:

1. Recall a time when you received a very different response than you expected. What was your reaction? Were you able to move forward, even though the situation wasn't what you anticipated?

2. Are you the type of person who can easily turn a small situation into a full-scale disaster? Who is someone you feel is able to keep perspective within their life?

3. When you think about the one necessary thing in your life, is this what you identified as the #1 item in the exercise in Chapter 7? Describe in a few sentences why you feel this is your one necessary thing.

4. As you reflect upon Mary's choice in her life, what encourages you? Disappoints you? Leaves you with more questions?

Prayer:

Holy God – Thank you for loving us so unconditionally. When we struggle to keep our most necessary thing at the top of our daily living, thank you for extending us grace. Speak to us as we make choices, and help us sort out this often confusing process. May we become people who can be still and truly know that You are God. Amen.

Part 3:

Help Towards Becoming a Recovering Martha

Chapter 10

Balance is a Four-Letter Word

Do not be shaped by this world; instead be changed within by a new way of thinking. Then you will be able to decide what God wants for you; you will know what is good and pleasing to him and what is perfect.

- Romans 12:2 (NCV)

Hubby Rick and I were attending our grandson's fifth birthday party. On a beautiful August day, the temperature was just right. The birthday boy, his brother, and a few young friends played in the yard. Little feet pattered in and out of the house. Squeals erupted as water balloons and other toys provided entertainment.

The party host's voice boomed from inside the house as she called out to the little people outside. As per her "normal" behavior, her rapid succession of four-letter words, which could have made a sailor blush, certainly made Rick and I squirm. We wanted to run over to all the little people, cover their ears, and hope they were so occupied with other things that the words had sailed right over their constantly moving heads.

True confession: yes, there are times I use inappropriate words. Most often, they come spilling out of my mouth because I feel the need to emphasize a point. I want the listener to understand my frustration and feelings. When this happens, I pray it's not done within a context where I am setting a bad example for little people.

Sometimes, inappropriate words contain more than four letters.

When leading worship, I enjoy gathering the littlest people together for a few minutes in what I call "Kid's Korner." One particular Sunday, we were exploring how sometimes yucky things happen to us. Rather than use the word "yucky," I chose to use a more profound word: Crappy. I should have taken the hint when a few of the kid's eyebrows raised at the first utterance. I didn't stop there though... No, I used it two more times with the kids. After Kid's Korner, the little people left worship for their specific Christian education time. Truth be known, I used the word "crappy" in the main message as well.

After worship, a 6-year-old girl marched right up to me. I knelt down so we were eye-to-eye. Her words stung as she said, "Pastor Dianne, you said a naughty word in church today. Not once. But three times. My parents don't let me use that word."

Immediately, I knew which word she was talking about. In her little world, this six-letter word was no different than the four-letter words we instruct our kids and grandchildren not to repeat in public and not-so-public places.

Suddenly, this esteemed pastor learned a lesson. As I apologized to this very aware girl and her parents, I became astutely conscious that what I say, the words I choose, and the context in which the words are spoken, influence people.

Knocking Balance Off Its Feet

For years, I idolized the word "balance." It was what I aspired to achieve and what my heart cried and yearned for. I convinced myself that achieving appropriate levels in all competing areas of my day-to-day activities would be like winning a Super Bowl trophy. Once achieved, I would have made it.

I began each New Year with one priority in mind: achieve balance. I willed myself to commit for the next 12 months to designing a life where I would have an appropriate work-play balance. Hubby Rick and I would achieve financial security, whatever that is. I would lose the evasive 20 pounds that has taken up residence on my body. I would spend 30minutes a day going through boxes of items that had been carted from house to house for decades. I would find meaningful time for my spouse, our families, and friends. I would develop a yet unnamed hobby to provide me space to decompress and find joy. Finally, I would put in the time to develop a strong spiritual bond between myself and God, which would be sustained by daily devotions and prayer time. Every. Single. Day. Of. The. Year.

By day two of this well-intended endeavor, I had lopped "balance" into the same category as the words that rolled off of the host's tongue at the birthday party. Crappy had a new best friend, and its name was balance. After yet another internal pep talk, I tried to convince myself that balance was possible. I just needed more devotion and willpower, that's all... I had hopped on the merry-go-round of trying to convince myself that balance was possible and attainable. I circled this ride for years and years, aspiring to achieve balance, but always feeling a thousand miles from it.

One day, I discovered an important lesson. A light switched on in my slow-to-recognize brain. *Balance was not realistic, possible, or achievable.* The sooner I hopped off the "balance" merry-go-round and said good-bye to the entire concept, the more peace I would experience in my life. I dug deep and realized balance is not fully obtainable. A life that is meaningful, joy-filled, and seasoned with lots of craziness and unpredictability is a more desirable aspiration.

This was also the day that I realized most hard-wired Martha's will always see balance as a four-letter word. For those Martha folks who think balance is the answer, can we put it on the "not necessary to be used" word shelf and let it hang out with those other words that make us cringe? As I vowed to move balance into the word graveyard, I dreamed about my own Mary Experiment. I shifted my focus from an unrealistic dream towards a possibility that could be life-giving, sustainable, and deeply meaningful.

Embracing a New Way of Thinking

Society tells us what our lives should look like: Perfect homes with beautifully manicured lawns. The entire family gathered around a home cooked meal where everyone replays the day's events. Kids who make wise choices. Spouses who work and have plenty of quality family time.

If you live this life, please send me your street address and zip code. I want to move in...

Meanwhile, please do not shame the majority of United States households, which treat balance like a four-letter word.

The day begins with the grind of getting everyone out the door. Multiple interruptions happen. Dinner is held in a moving vehicle, provided by the local fast food drive-thru. Exhausted parents tackle homework and attending activities. Bank accounts indicate insufficient funds... again. Just before throwing yourself into an unmade bed with dirty sheets, tomorrow's calendar indicates another jam-packed, non-stop day on deck.

Balance begins as a good intention that never seems to make it out of the starting blocks. Why? Because balance is subjective. What may feel like balance to you may not feel like balance to me. For that one minute of that one day, when balance almost feels attainable, it only takes one phone call, text message, or email to throw everything into a rollercoaster ride once again. While we may feel there is adequate balance in one area of our lives, another area feels like a hot mess.

The struggle to feel like I have achieved a level of balance is just not a reality for me. After years and years of doing the same thing over and over and expecting different results, I reminded myself this is the definition of insanity.

Pause for just a minute. Have you ever aspired to have balance in your life? How did this work for you? What challenges did you find in trying to achieve balance?

Shifting Away from Balance

So, if balance is not the solution, what is?

Let's go back to what God inspired Paul to write about this topic:

> *Do not be shaped by this world; instead be changed within by a new way of thinking. Then you will be able to decide what God wants for you; you will know what is good and pleasing to him and what is perfect.*
>
> **- Romans 12:2 (NCV)**

When I was ordained as a pastor, I was asked to select one Bible verse that resonated with my life. This is the verse I chose. For me, this verse says that God knows I need to live in the world. I'll be faced with lots of choices and options. Some will be great. Some will be, well, not so much. As easy as it is to be influenced by society, culture, and the world, please shift your way of thinking, Paul says. Rather than seeking what everyone else is doing or saying or choosing, go back to God. Consult with God first. Then, it will become clear the path God prefers you to follow.

Theologian Karl Barth described it this way. He advised young theologians "to take your Bible and take your newspaper, and read both. But interpret newspapers from your Bible." In essence, Barth is saying we need today's news along with the Bible to help us understand today's world. We can't isolate ourselves into one camp. It's best to keep a foot in both arenas.

While this sounds good in theory, finding God's will for your life is tricky. Well, at least it is for me. I pray and journal and ask God for clarity and direction. Sometimes it comes easily, other times, it is so evasive. Or maybe I just miss the indications. While Paul says to seek God first, I also know that God uses those around us as messengers as well. This has happened multiple times in my life, including some rather profound and dramatic ways. Other times, God has spoken to me through a person in a still, quiet voice. Either way, I should be diligent in confirming this as God's path for me. Once I do, then it's time to make strides towards it.

This Mary Experiment came out of the realization that maintaining my typical workload and schedule was not sustainable for the long-term. When I concluded that balance was a four-letter word, I shifted towards wanting more peace in my life. Daily joy. A conviction that I didn't have to do everything I could do; instead, I should be picky and choose only the things that God ordained me to do. This meant giving up some things I really, really liked to do, like prepare a message for weekly Sunday worship. But it also meant that I would be able to pull together all the wild and crazy experiences I have had, and rope them together in a way that hopefully others could relate to. Resonate with. Maybe even use to contemplate making changes in their own lives.

If I am brutally honest, this road has not always gone well. Too often, I became distracted by other things rather than fully engaging in what I felt God had called me to truly focus on. Some days, I was inspired to leave balance in the word graveyard and focus on joy, peace, and contentment. Other days, I let myself disguise balance in a variety of ways before realizing that, once again, I had allowed myself to try the balance route with no success.

Shifting Away from Balance

Before I could completely let go of balance, I had to find new words to define my life. I needed a Plan B. Once I determined these, I could finally let balance stay at a wayside and focus on a new definition for how I choose to live my life.

This has led me to daily affirm joy, gratitude, and contentment.

I no longer strive to be "the best" at everything I do and attempt. Life is ratcheted down into something that feels more doable, realistic, and achievable. Internally, I feel more grounded. Fresh. Less pressed to be something other than what God longs for me to be.

I do not aspire to be the person whose name everybody knows. I just want to be a woman who quietly sees opportunities and affects change and impact where I can. Hubby Rick and I pray that we shine just a little bit of God's kingdom and God's love into someone's life, if only for today.

Gratitude, joy, and contentment are not four-letter words for me. When I center myself with comforting words, as well as have confidence that I'm seeking God's will for my life today, I can lay my head on the pillow at the end of the day and say to God, "It was enough. I did my best. Now, You take it and do the rest. Fix my mistakes. Remind me that tomorrow, we get to do it all over again. Thanks for being with me on this journey. Amen."

I still struggle with assessing whether or not what I did was "enough." There are days when I could easily use four-letter words to describe how I feel. Yet, I pray that my attitude towards life does not make God want to blush. When I stop relying on myself for every good result and outcome, I am assured that God can take whatever I did, or didn't do, and still make something beautiful out of it.

As I dumped "balance" to the side of the road, I caught myself finding glimpses of moving away from an over-extended Martha lifestyle towards hints of more Mary-influence in my life. The probability of ever becoming a dyed-in-the-wool Mary is not realistic. I'm just not wired that way. When I allow myself to tie together extended moments of Mary-ness into my life, I began to feel like I am moving towards who God calls me to be.

Reflection Questions:

1. Ponder your view of balance. Do you feel it is obtainable? Why or why not?

2. Are you more influenced by society or the Bible? How can or do you incorporate both in your decisions for how you live your life?

3. Choose a few words that you long to define your life. Do you feel you embrace these words on a daily basis? If so, how?

4. What would you like to accomplish as a result of reading *The Mary Experiment*? How might your life look different? How would you feel different?

Prayer:

Dear God – Forgive us for the times when we have yearned for something of this world, rather than what we find in You. Assure us that a less scattered feeling and mode of living is possible through You. Amen.

CHAPTER 11

Life's Boundaries

So, Jesus said to them, "When you lift up the Son of Man, you will know that I am He. You will know that these things I do are not by my own authority, but that I say only what the Father has taught me. The One who sent me is with me. I always do what is pleasing to Him, so He has not left me alone."

- John 8:28-29 (NCV)

I remember a day, long, long ago, when television stations were not up all night. They shut down. Turned off. Took a break.

At about midnight, local stations played the National Anthem while a flag rippled quietly in the background. When the song was over, the screen became a buzz of white static noise with no picture until dawn the following morning.

Yes, those were the days before satellite television and around the clock news. When reruns were rare, and only for classic shows like Hogan's Heroes and M.A.S.H. If you missed a show during its actual time slot, you picked up a phone attached to the wall, waited for the person on your party line to complete their conversation, and made a call to a friend to hear what you missed.

I know, I am as old as the dinosaurs.

But for several hours, the television station went off-air. The world slept. There was a start time and an end time. There were boundaries.

Nowadays, society has no boundaries left. We have raised generations of kids who know television only as a 24-hour experience. With hundreds of channels to choose from, it is still amazing how often we say, "But there's nothing good to watch." Nonetheless, we plop down in front of these rectangle boxes and watch hours of comedy, action thrillers, and reality television to escape our overloaded, overextended, and overcommitted lives - especially when they feel like they are reeling out of control.

After television stations stopped taking breaks, it seemed like the rest of society dropped their boundaries as well. We began to foster the endless need to keep going, doing, and working.

Let's be clear. Previous generations worked hard. For practical reasons, these people realized that life did not need to run 24/7 for days on end. There were starts and stops to days, weeks, and months. Life included clearer boundaries and expectations.

Today, our lives are often filled with laundry-lists of "must-do's" for every day of the week, with little or no thought about restoring our hearts, souls, and minds. We foster overscheduled lives for ourselves and children. Afraid we will miss out on something, we spend more time reading what is happening in other people's lives than connecting with the person sitting next to us.

Walk into a room where people are waiting. Every single person has their eyes glued to a little piece of equipment in front of their noses, oblivious to what might be happening in the lives of people around them. The man sitting in muddy work boots wearing a reflective top knows he won't be able to make the mortgage payment because his family is financially overextended. It is easier to live vicariously through professional athletes than make difficult choices about spending habits. The perfectly coiffed woman is falling apart internally from anxiety and depression. She's afraid to let a piece of her armor down, for fear that she will be judged as not being "good enough."

With no sacred time of the week remaining anymore, the only possible way to carve out such times is if we are intentional. When I have tried to impose a boundary or two with youth, teens, or adults about screen time, in an effort to engage those who are together, there is whining and protest. I hear, "But everyone else has their phone," or "This is too important for me to miss," or "You can't tell me what to do."

Yes, sometimes I am the offender as well. I catch myself quickly looking something up on my phone rather than letting a question go unanswered. Or I sneak in a quick look on a social media account, hoping someone will not notice. More than once, I have been busted, as I should have been.

It is difficult to reel back lowered boundaries. Busyness can be so addictive that we forget what truly is important. We scurry through our to-do lists and focus on crossing off one more item, not realizing that we failed to be present when a ministry opportunity was right in front of us. We step right over life's sacred moments without fully drinking them in, because we have moved onto the next thing and missed God's little blessing in our lives in the moment.

Making drastic choices will not get you on a best parent/sibling/spouse/friend list. How can we try and live with our unlimited sources of technology in one hand, while holding God's scriptural encouragements in the other?

It requires a bit of creative thinking and effort.

"Too Much" Can be Sin

The idea of "too much" as sin was a new concept for me. My "too much" was easily justified by, "I want to do the best job that I can," or "Someone has to do this," or "There will be time to rest when I die." The opportunity cost of overextending myself through time, talents, and gifts simply never entered my thought process.

When I was in seminary, I enrolled in a class called *Redeeming the Routines of Ministry and Life.* The class's premise was to assist students to develop a theology and ethic of work and leisure. Professor Dr. Colyer encouraged students to develop a healthy understanding of how our backgrounds affect our attitudes towards work and leisure, diagram how we prefer our lives to be, and implement routines to help maintain a life-long commitment to ministry and life.

In this class, I was challenged to rethink how I define work. Typically, we think of "work" as an activity whose goal is to create something. We think of "work" as what we do for compensation.

The opposite of work is leisure. These are the things we choose to do when we have the freedom to make choices. It's the fun things we enjoy doing and yearn to have more time to do so.

Unfortunately, Martha's are ingrained with the idea that we must work first and play second. However, Martha's often impose so much work in their lives that there is little time left for play.

Think about the last week of your life. When did you play? What leisure activities did you choose to do in your play? How did you feel after you allowed yourself to play?

Reinterpreting Work and Leisure

In his book, *The Work of the Spirit*, Miroslav Volf challenges readers to not see "work" and "leisure" as polar opposites. "The same activity can be both work and leisure," he says. Volf champions the idea that those who feel most satisfied in life are able to move as many commitments in their lives towards a middle position between work and leisure. He calls these semi-leisure activities.

Rather than seeing leisure as "wasting time," we can embrace fun and play activities as where our heart often yearns to be. We redefine "work" as what tugs at our heart and what is most important to us, rather than what we get paid to do. Instead of organizing our lives around our paid work, we prioritize our lives around the fun and exciting activities where we play. This is how we move towards a middle ground between work and leisure.

When we move more daily activities to a position between work and leisure, the lines between the two become blurry. While this may initially feel uncomfortable, when we allow this to change, amazing results can happen.

Maybe Martha loved to make homemade soap, scented with lavender or lemon. Possibly, she sold little bars at the neighborhood market. She also longed to give a gift to company when they visited. Would she have time to make soap? If Martha sees making soap as restorative and relaxing, she turns soap making into a semi-leisure activity.

When we shift our thinking and see certain responsibilities as something we choose to do more for fun than work, we discover our sweet spots. We find a place where our soul sings because it is happy. Here, we partner with God to do the very best things God intends for us to do. Our hearts are filled as we make contributions to God's kingdom and fill our happiness tanks at the same time.

When this happens, we discover a partnership with the Spirit where we truly feel blessed. We find gratitude in life's little things rather than struggling with whether we've ever quite "made it." We enjoy today, the present, as truly a gift from God. We also discover that we do not need to redeem our lives because God the Father, the Son, and the Holy Spirit, has already done this for us.

Knowing When Enough is Enough

Ten people were gathered around my dining room table. They were from one of the two churches where I was serving as pastor. Labeled the "Long-Range Planning Team," this group's job was to find ways for two small and struggling churches to position themselves for a future where they would be viable and sustainable long-term.

We had spent months coming up with ideas, checklists, and thoughts of how God was calling them into their next phase of ministry. We were reviewing this information one last time before taking it to each individual church board for approval.

I wanted to think this team had been following the Spirit. We had asked for guidance and input at the beginning and closing of each meeting. Lots of time and energy had happened to reach this point. We also knew the real work of implementation was just around the corner.

Before we reached final consensus, Jeff spoke up and voiced the thoughts of many others around the table. Gently, he told this Martha-like pastor that all the information looked good and sounded great. But when was enough going to be enough? Every person present was already tapped out in terms of time commitments. Who was going to implement these wonderful ideas when most active participants were already doing their max?

Jeff inquired thoughtfully about whether God appreciates what the churches were already doing. Shouldn't being a Christian not just be based on a series of actions and checklists? Speaking for himself, as an overextended man who struggled with whether or not he was doing enough, Jeff asked, "Sometimes, doesn't God think what we're doing is already enough?"

I found myself squirming in my chair, but not because Jeff's question addressed the validity of months and months of work. His question was one my heart had been asking for years and years. One I could not adequately answer.

Often, Martha's do not answer a question unless they already know the answer. They anticipate what result actions will produce in advance. They are driven by ensuring their effort will be rewarded. Mary's are not nearly as concerned about results, because they are more comfortable with God taking their efforts and moving them beyond their abilities.

Volf says that too often, we develop a moral and ethical view of work independently from a moral view of our private lives. When God lives in us, God is part of our whole reality. Separate worldviews of work and private lives no longer exist, because God becomes part of our entire being. We see our short earthly lives as preparation for our much longer eternal life.

When we move towards a more holistic view of work and leisure, our lives are not defined by our job. Being an accountant, a teacher, a tradesperson, or a stay-at-home parent is not what most accurately defines our life. Rather, being a disciple of Jesus Christ is where our identity lies. We allow our greatest fulfillment to come out of activity that satisfies us because it is centered in our understanding of being a beloved child of God. We find more connecting points in our daily activities. We create a sense that what we are doing is enough... for ourselves and for God.

Martha's Need Margin

But let's be real. For Martha's, maintaining this attitude is challenging. Too often, Martha's are so busy that they miss God's wonderful appearances in their lives. By constantly doing, we fail to allow for adequate margin to repair from an abundance of activity and regroup for what lies ahead.

In his book, *Margin: Restoring Emotional, Physical, Financial and Time Reserves to Overloaded Lives,* Richard A. Swenson, M.D. encourages folks to escape their suffocating schedules and gain freedom in their lives. He calls this margin. Margin is "the space between our load and our limits... the gap between rest and exhaustion, the space between breathing freely and suffocating. Margin is the opposite of overload."

As a private practice physician, Swenson saw marginless people nearly every fifteen minutes a day in his office. These exhausted and hurting patients don't know what margin is. Most do not realize that their pain directly relates to an absence of margin. If an over-extended Martha paid him a visit at his doctor's office, he would encourage them to inject a healthy dose of margin into their lives.

I view margin as living in the same place as semi-leisure activities. It's where life activity hovers between work and leisure. Where we feel contentment and peace. The place where we partner with God in the daily choices that we make. Martha's who are able to add some Mary to their personality, purposefully add margin to their lives.

Jesus said it this way:

> *"You will know that these things I do are not by my own authority, but that I say only what the Father has taught me. The One who sent me is with me. I always do what is pleasing to Him, so He has not left me alone."*

- John 8:28b-29 (NCV)

The Jewish people are trying to figure out who this man named Jesus is. He tells the local Jewish church leaders that they have no clue where He came from or where He is going. As He says that He stands with His Father, the church leaders naively ask who His father is. Jesus reiterates that if they listened to what He said about who He was, they would know His Father.

Again, the Jews asked who Jesus is. Jesus replies with the same answer. "I only speak what the Father has taught me. I do what pleases my Father."

The difference between Jesus and us, is that Jesus always knew that whatever He did *was* enough. He never second-guessed whether He had healed enough people, or fed enough mouths, or taught enough life lessons. Whatever He did was simply enough. After tough days of ministry, Jesus specifically sought margin within His life. He went away and prayed. He'd send the disciples on their way so He could rest and restore himself. He blew the dust off of His sandals repeatedly, knowing that every person He came in contact with was not ready to hear His message. And He simply moved on.

Ms. Martha-me is not so sure of herself. I'm not that comfortable turning over what I have done into the more capable hands of God, and letting God bless and anoint my efforts. I keep thinking, "If I just do this little bit more, then..."

I've misplaced awe for the Kingdom of God and knowing that the Lord can take whatever I do and multiply it into something more - if I'd only trust God to do so.

Jesus saw the crowds on a hillside one day. He sat with them and taught. Notice He didn't say:

> *Blessed are the busy addicts. You will rack up lots of points to get into heaven.*
>
> *Blessed are those with expectations of outdoing everyone else. I applaud your drive and determination.*
>
> *Blessed are the Martha's of the world. You outshine all others.*

Instead, Jesus blessed the humble, the meek, and the merciful. He celebrated those whose hearts are fully turned towards God and seek opportunities to hear God daily. He preferred the less skilled over the over-functioning one, who is blurry-eyed and dull to God's presence in their lives. He longed for people to listen more to God's voice than those who speak loud enough to have their own voice heard above all others.

How can we restore our awe of God and God's kingdom? Shift our best time and energy from simply performing a job, towards doing the most important things God calls us to do. Learn to partner the areas of our lives that bring us joy within more of our daily activities. Desire for margin to fill us rather than activity that drains us.

In seminary, I completed all the classwork required for the *Redeeming the Routines* class. I finished the required lessons and papers and wrote out a detailed theology, vision, goals, checklists, and priorities in multiple areas of my life. Dr. Colyer applauded my efforts and awarded me an A+ in the class.

While the class materials were stellar, my application of them for the next decade-and-a-half were mediocre at best. I struggled with knowing when enough was enough. I couldn't let myself turn over ministry and projects and life situations, and allow for God to bless and anoint them. Margin was most often a little empty space around my long to-do lists. I struggled with fully incorporating a theology of moral and ethical values that infiltrated all areas of my life. As much as I wanted to let my life have times of silence, like the television stations of my youth, this recovering Martha has kept the lights on way too often.

Reflection Questions:

1. How do you shut off work and allow for leisure time in your life?

2. Who is someone you know that can honestly say, "My job isn't work because I love it so much?" What allows their "work" to feel that way?

3. Describe something in your life that falls into the semi-leisure area. How does this activity bring margin back into your life?

4. Do you struggle with allowing your 'enough' to be enough for God? Why or why not?

Prayer:

Dear God – Too often, we view life from the shallow end of the pool, where work becomes the defining aspect of our lives. Challenge us to explore how we can find more opportunities to combine what our heart yearns to do with aspects of our lives that are life-giving. May we not feel ashamed of building margin into our lives, but allow for space where we can simply be in awe of Your kingdom. Amen.

Chapter 12

It Begins with Gratitude

Let the word of Christ dwell in you richly; teach and admonish one another in all wisdom; and with gratitude in your hearts sing psalms, hymns, and spiritual songs to God.

- Colossians 3:16 (NRSV)

I see myself as a glass-half-full kind of gal. The kind of person who makes lemonade out of any lemony event.

One summer, I was part of the adult team on a weeklong youth mission trip just outside of Washington D.C. We stayed and helped at a youth camp for underprivileged kids. Youth from our group were their counselors. They played games, made crafts, ate lunch, and participated in activities with the kids. The camp provided a safe environment for youth who often lived in less than stable situations.

The adult leaders helped with a variety of projects. Sometimes we helped in the kitchen. We took turns accompanying our youth to a homeless shelter, where we prepared the noon meal and cleaned the bunk house. It had been above 95 degrees with equally high humidity the entire week. In the blistering heat, we helped with camp maintenance projects. Our housing arrangements were tents, which felt stifling in the heat. By the end of the week, we were tired and ready to go home.

On our last workday, some adults laid five yards of small rock onto a walking path, using only a small wheelbarrow and five-gallon buckets. It was exhausting work. Just after lunch, the adults met quickly to determine who would finish the walking path project. Of course, Ms. Martha wanted it completely finished before our vans rolled away from the camp.

Our adult leader was not so sure. The heat? The humidity? The physical demands? He encouraged others to veto my plan. I pleaded with the other leaders. This was our last opportunity to finish this project, one we had been working on all week. Wouldn't it be nice to drive away from the camp knowing the walking path project was completed? With over half of the rock already moved, it would take just a couple of hours to finish.

Clearly not amused with my enthusiasm, the leader quipped, "Dianne, do you always have to be so dang Pollyannaish? The entire week, you've always pointed out the good in something. Constantly encouraging for more and more. Isn't it time to stop doing? I'm tired and don't see finishing this project as something very fun."

Honestly, I have not always been Pollyannaish. There have been plenty of times when I focused more on the negative than on the positive. It makes my heart sad when I recall the various times when I have let a bad attitude cloud my perspective.

When this Martha gets overwhelmed and tired, or I feel like things are spinning out of control, it is easy to revert to the negative rather than focusing on the positive. Thankfully, I have a person in my life who often points out how blessed I am.

Hubby Rick looks at every sunset and is amazed at God's creation. Rick works nights and drives truck. Sometimes, he sends me a text message and asks if I have seen the "awesome sunset;" a sunset he sees through his windshield. Too often, I am sitting at my desk, oblivious to the beauty right outside the window.

A woman once told me, "I have never met a couple who are more opposite than you and Rick." I plan and prepare. He flies by the seat of his pants. I anticipate and expect. He lets things happen as they may. My calendar contains everything in my life, and I would be lost without it. Rick doesn't own one.

When someone asks Rick how he is, his standard answer is: "Better than I deserve." For years, Rick has encouraged me to stop and smell the roses. Be grateful for what we have. Appreciate our health, security, and where we are in this stage of our lives. As much as I have wanted to believe I was grateful for all of this and more, honestly, I haven't been.

Yes, there are glimmers of gratefulness in my life. I appreciate a husband who has put up with my crazy schedule for years. I treasure having been raised in a family that taught me the value of a hard day's work. I never worry about opening up the pantry or checkbook and wondering if our next meal or gas bill will be covered.

Yet, do I stop and see the beauty around me? Do I say that I do this, but in reality, I don't? Do I write thank you notes consistently because I want to express my gratitude, or just because my mom taught me to do so? Are my days filled because of all the great things I have the opportunity to do... or do I dread each day because "there is no way I'll ever get this all done?"

If I were honest, I would say that my appreciation of gratitude is mostly skin deep. While I talk about it, encourage others to embody it, and seem that I value gratitude, deep-down, I have often been a gratitude hypocrite. The person who signs her emails with, "Blessings – Dianne" has not always counted every blessing in her life.

Too often, I view blessings as curses - another sermon to write, another email to follow-up with, and another meeting to prepare for. Another disagreement to negotiate. Another day with 16 hours of work that needs to be squeezed into 12 hours. Another missed dinner with my husband because something else was deemed "more important."

There's a long list of psychologists and researchers who agree that a shift in how a person understands gratitude can make a significant difference in our happiness level. The Roman philosopher Cicero had this figured out a long time ago. He said, "Gratitude is not only the greatest of virtues, but the parent of all others."

Why has it taken me so long to figure this out?

It Starts with Gratitude

Gratitude is a Christian value. It's the widow who drops her last two small coins into the offering box. It's the Samaritan leper, one of ten whom Jesus heals, the only one that came back and offered thanks. Unfortunately, the other nine missed Christ's blessing, all because they failed to express gratitude. It's Mary expressing deep honor and gratitude for being chosen as the mother of the Savior, rather than contemplating the shame, disrespect, and judgment she will endure.

The most poignant example of gratitude comes from Jesus. After being whipped, beaten, and hung on a cross to die, he prays for all the people who did these things to him. With this prayer, "Father, forgive these people! They don't know what they're doing," Jesus expresses the deepest gratitude a person can express.

Gratitude has been on my radar screen for a long time. Yet, my Martha personality required a shift in how I embrace and experience gratitude. My concept of gratitude needed to be *reframed.*

Dr. Robert Emmons of the University of California-Davis has become one of the world's leading experts on gratitude. He says people don't need good events in their lives to feel gratitude. Grateful people reframe whatever happens to them. Rather than focus on what they lack, grateful people make sure they see the good in what they have.[5]

When a Martha begins to find gratitude in their life regularly, they discover more Mary-ness in their lives. This is one of the great gifts Hubby Rick, a self-proclaimed Mary, brings into my life. Moments of gratitude become moments of margin for me. It helps me see the "work" that I do as part of my giftedness and calling, which helps me appreciate my work more as a semi-leisure activity. I now love taking the lemons in my daily life and turning them into lemonade.

Reframing doesn't happen overnight. When I intentionally choose to honor gratitude in my life, I celebrate small blessings. As I reframe an overly busy-Martha life, gratitude becomes a strong and sustaining value of my daily being.

Slowing Down and Finding Gratitude

How does reframing happen in daily life? Here are a few seemingly simple, yet intentional, ways we can reframe our lives.

---

[5] Janice Kaplan, *The Gratitude Diaries*, (Dutton: New York), 16.

See God in the Everyday.

Yes, it really is this simple. Ann Voskamp shared how identifying *One Thousand Gifts* changed her perspective on waking up to God's everyday blessings in her life. She challenged herself to find 1,000 ways God has blessed her life. By giving thanks for the life she already had, Voskamp discovered she had the life she'd always wanted. She encourages others to try the same exercise.

My friend Carlene introduced me to Voskamp's book. Carlene's youngest son died from brain cancer when he was only 18. We met some time after this, and together Carlene and I shared heartaches and joys over breakfast and coffee. I watched Carlene go through many devastating challenges with grace. She experienced her own bouts of cancer. A short 19 months after the death of her youngest son, Carlene's eldest son was killed in a motorcycle accident. The week of his funeral, Carlene was scheduled to meet with an oncologist to explore ways to slow her own cancer.

When Carlene brought me Voskamp's book, the irony was not lost. This woman, who could have been bitter about many things, was reframing her life and counting her blessings. Over eggs and rewarmed cups of coffee, Carlene explained how she was giving this book to loved ones. She wanted part of her legacy to be helping others experience blessings in their lives. In her life, she challenged herself to be filled with deep appreciation for all God had given her. Rather than focus on her losses, Carlene made lemonade. For Carlene, every day was truly a present - a gift. Her glass was half-full.

We choose whether to embrace today as a gift, a present, and live it filled with gratitude. Or angst.

Keep a Gratitude Journal

For years, I have journaled. My journals are filled with lots of things: how the lives of students I taught changed while serving as a missionary; details from when Rick and I dated; records of wonderful or challenging days of pastoral ministry. Lots and lots of prayers.

To incorporate gratitude in my journal, I often answer these statements:

1. Three things I am grateful for:
2. One thing I am anxious about:
3. Three things I want to accomplish today:

Ms. Martha loves to identify where I want the day to go, and I usually have more than three things listed. However, when I discern today's priorities after I have reflected upon what I am grateful for, I tend to focus more on what I *have*, before what I feel must be done.

Periodically, I look back through my journals and recall how much I have to be thankful for. I see where God is working in and through my life.

Find Gratitude in the Ordinary

Too often, we overlook gratitude in the mundane. We do many things automatically and without thinking. Sometimes, we cease to respond to a stimulus after repeated occurrences. At this point, something may no longer seem relevant.

Habituation is what allows a parent to quietly watch television or eat a meal while their child screams. It's what happens when couples forget what they thought was special in their relationship. Soon, complacency and expectation lead to a lack of gratitude.

How can we stop habituation and find gratitude in our lives? It is finding comfort in the simple things. A quick thank you when it's freezing cold outside, but the car still starts. A "Praise the Lord!" when hot water comes out of the faucet. A word of grace before diving into dinner.

Does this mean we go through our days shouting "Alleluia!" and "Amen!?" Your office mates might find it a bit annoying when you give thanks for the phone ringing... again. Your children or grandchildren may not quite understand why you break into song when you safely stop at the yellow light. Yet, why don't we give thanks for the ordinary aspects of our daily lives? Does a special event have to occur for us to be grateful?

Pastor Adam Hamilton from the Church of the Resurrection in Kansas City, MO, shares how after Christmas, he prays over every Christmas card that he receives. He reads each card and says a short prayer for each family represented by a card.

For the last several years, I have practiced this. A week or two after Christmas, I grab the basket in which I've thrown the various cards and notes that Rick and I have received. In a comfortable chair, I re-read every card. With more time to study the shared pictures and words, I slow down and remember why we receive a card from this family. Then, I lay my hand on the card and pray for this family.

Explore other ways this can be used in your ordinary world. Before putting a note or card in the mail, lay your hand on each card, expressing gratitude for this family's presence in your life. While paying bills, expressing gratitude for the funds to pay each bill and the received benefit from this expense.

While cooking dinner, give thanks for the farmers who produced the food you will enjoy. While using an appliance, express gratitude for electricity. While pulling out of the driveway, be thankful for the safe vehicle you have to drive.

These are very simple, quick ways to infuse gratitude in your life and experience a little less habituation. Ordinary expressions of gratitude do not take extra time, but they can help reframe your day. They also allow us to focus on what we have, versus what we think we want.

A Gratitude Journal for a Loved One

When 2017 began, I bought a small calendar book that I labeled *Hubby Rick's Journal.* The calendar provided a half-page for each day. Throughout the year, I wrote an expression of gratitude for each day. With just one or two sentences, I captured something from the day that I wanted Rick to know I appreciated. At the time, we didn't see each other every day because of our schedules. On the days we didn't see each other, I expressed a hope for the future, something from the past, or simply honored him with a gratitude statement.

The journal was a daily reminder of how much I appreciate my husband. At the end of the year, I shared the journal with Rick. Before giving it to him, I realized that this exercise was more for me than what he would read. I needed to discover a daily affirmation and way to be grateful for my spouse and our lives.

A personal gratitude journal can be used for a variety of people. Choose a person who you want to deepen your affection and gratitude towards. See how you feel after keeping a gratitude journal for them.

Allow God to Surprise You

Sometimes God has answered one of my prayers in a very unique and special way. Rather than becoming frustrated that my prayer was answered quite differently from what I expected, I try to remind myself that God knows more of my needs than I do.

In the 1990's, I spent a year overseas teaching English as a missionary in the country of Kazakhstan. I lived there in a tumultuous time, when Kazakhstan was figuring out how to be a country autonomous from the Soviet Union. Things like regular payment for employment were not established.

I lived and worked with another American teacher, Amy. We taught English at a state university and were considered state employees. We received some salary shortly after we arrived in early September. We had not been paid again as Thanksgiving rolled around, even though our contract with the university stipulated that we be paid monthly. It had been nearly three months since we had been paid a stipend.

On Monday nights, Amy and I spent time studying the Bible and praying together. On the Monday before Thanksgiving, Amy was very specific about her prayer request. We *needed* to be paid. I would have to approach the university department head and insist we receive our stipend immediately. We bathed this plan in prayer.

On Tuesday evenings, I visited the apartment of our American friends, Jim and Grace. They had three elementary-aged children. I earned extra money by giving their two daughters weekly piano lessons.

On this cold November evening, it started snowing as I walked to Jim and Grace's apartment. Even though we lived in Kazakhstan's largest city of Almaty, there was no snow removal equipment, sand, or salt. With even a small snowfall, cars would easily get stuck. The lack of salt, combined with most cars having nearly bald tires, led to havoc in the streets.

After piano lessons, Grace insisted on driving me home. This particular evening, I knew that I could walk almost as fast as driving. But Grace insisted on taking me home. At our apartment building, Grace opened the back of their Russian-made vehicle, where two boxes sat. She instructed me to grab a box. We each hiked a box up the four flights of stairs to our apartment. Grace wished me a Happy Thanksgiving and left.

When Amy and I opened the boxes, we were overwhelmed. They were filled with food. Canned goods, a highly coveted jar of peanut butter, a can of U.S. turkey. Enough food to last for a few weeks. Jim and Grace's generosity spoke volumes. While they were not specifically aware of our non-payment situation, somehow, they just knew. I discovered an important lesson that evening. Often, God truly knows our needs and will answer them in a creative way. We didn't get paid that week, but we still received exactly what we needed.

Sometimes, Martha's can be so insistent. We think we know exactly what we need. Thankfully, God knows our needs more than we do ourselves.

Hit the Pause Button

Too often, the Martha in me just wants to do, do, do. Sometimes, I just need to be, be, be.

When I allow myself to hear God's Spirit in my life, telling me that I need to slow down, I am seldom disappointed with the results. Unfortunately, I sometimes do not allow myself to be still enough to hear God speak to me. When I hear God challenge me to slow down, can I allow myself to let Mary creep in and hit the pause button? Can I allow myself to just be?

Hubby Rick's mom had been in a nursing home for several months. She wanted to spend her final days in her own home. While Rick's dad was present, Rick and I felt his mom needed additional care. After prayer and contemplation, Rick and I decided that I would step away from pastoral ministry and help provide care for Ersel. Once we had Rick's parents and sisters on board with this, I requested a year of family leave.

Before this, Rick had been staying at his parents' house several days a week. Basically, I moved in, and we stayed with them most of the week.

When we agreed to this arrangement, we did not know if Ersel would live another six weeks, six months, or six years. At the time, Rick and I were confident this was the right decision. It would be a time that we would relish and appreciate. It was also the first time in our married life that we saw each other every day of the week.

Ersel lived about five months. These months were an opportunity for my soul to be fed by things different from my normal pastor life. I spent wonderful time with my very gracious mother-in-law in the last days of her life. Rick and I discovered that seeing each other every day was a good thing. We saw more of our three grandchildren, who lived close by.

Hitting the pause button does not have to be this significant. Sometimes, it's taking 15 minutes and having a lovely conversation with a friend. Other times, it's pausing life for an hour or two and helping someone with a task. Maybe it is allowing yourself to provide respite or relief for another person. Sometimes, it's an overnight to reconnect with your spouse.

I have been the very appreciative recipient of those who have hit the pause button and helped me in some way. Their commitment to do so speaks volumes. It is difficult to accurately convey my deep appreciation when this happens.

I am also keenly aware that I have chosen to ignore opportunities to hit the pause button, and later regretted it. The person who I'd always *meant* to visit and never did, until it was too late. The five-minute call that could have been made and wasn't. Too often, my Martha side decides that some piece of work is more important than upholding a relationship. But when I have listened to the inner voice telling me to pause and be still, I've seldom been disappointed. Almost always, I walk away from these situations with more gratitude in my heart.

As the last hours of the mission trip dwindled down, another adult and I completed moving the stone and finished the walking path. Maybe my Martha attitude just could not leave without finishing the path. Yet the gratitude expressed when the camp directors saw the completed project confirmed that the right decision was made.

Gratitude can easily be found in our lives when we simply reframe a situation. It's choosing to make lemonade from the lemons that could leave us bitter. It's being committed to living as glass-half-full kind of people. Maybe the French novelist Marcel Proust said it best: "The real voyage of discovery consists not in seeking new lands, but seeing with new eyes."

Reflection Questions:

1. Who is someone that truly appreciates the little things in life? How does their attitude affect you?

2. How would you define gratitude? On a scale of 1 to 10, with 10 being the highest, where would you rank yourself as a person who embodies gratitude in their daily life?

3. How do you honor and celebrate gratitude in your daily life? Do these actions help you slow down your Martha-like tendencies?

4. Expressing gratitude can often be done within the confines of our regular days. How could you incorporate new ways to express gratitude in your ordinary days?

5. Answer these three questions in your life:
    1. Three things I am grateful for:
    2. One thing I am anxious about:
    3. Three things I want to accomplish today:

Prayer:

Holy God – Forgive us for the times when we have focused more on what we don't have rather than expressing gratitude for what we do have. Thank you for providing for all of our needs, as well as so many of our wants. Help us bathe our days with gratitude. As we discover new opportunities to express gratitude for each day, may these become moments when we slow down and truly appreciate our lives. Amen.

Chapter 13

Application for 21st Century Souls

I don't really understand myself, for I want to do what is right, but I don't do it. Instead, I do what I hate.

- Romans 7:15 (NLT)

In the last four decades of my life, I have lost hundreds of pounds.

I've also *gained* hundreds of pounds. Unfortunately, I've gained more pounds than I have lost.

I have struggled with weight nearly my entire life. There have been very few years when an elusive number of pounds have not taken up residence on my body and decided they really like the provided environment. I have never been one of those people who could eat whatever I wanted. Just looking at a sweet dessert is the same as depositing it right onto my hips. It's amazing how simply thinking about some decadent meal makes the scale increase.

It would be impossible for me to guess how many times I have promised myself that my eating habits will be different tomorrow. Often, I say to myself,

"Today, you will get your eating under control. You will avoid sugar, cut back on carbs, and only eat when you are REALLY hungry."

Most of those days? My willpower lasted until about noon. Or until I decided ice cream sounded really good. Or the brownies I walked by were irresistible.

For some people, willpower may be enough. If you are one of those people, I envy you. I yearn for your commitment.

For the rest of us? We need an alternative. We need something more than willpower, because simple willpower constantly fails us. We look for something that will help us get over life's humps. We long to be the best version of ourselves that we can be. We accept a holistic understanding of failure that says when it happens, we have not failed but simply encountered a challenge. These challenges help us grow, mature, and discover something new about ourselves.

If willpower doesn't work for you, I pray you find comfort in knowing that you are not the only one who needs something more than willpower.

More Than Willpower

The Apostle Paul is a very colorful guy in the New Testament. After spending years heckling Jesus' followers and making sure they were persecuted, Paul suddenly had a life-changing event. It took a blinding light and three days of lost eyesight to shift his attention from putting Christ-followers in prison to preaching the good news of Jesus. After Paul's epiphany, the disciples and other believers were leery of his intentions and commitment. Eventually, Paul convinced others of his sincerity. As he shared the story of Jesus Christ, Paul became a foremost missionary of the early Christian church.

To do this, Paul turned his life upside down. He gave up a lucrative job and became a traveling tent maker. No longer with a home, he journeyed from city to city. Paul started many early Christian churches and instructed new believers about how to live their lives dedicated to God. When early believers disagreed and argued over whether or not to eat meat sacrificed to idols, they wrote Paul for guidance and direction. He became the poster child for how to live your life as a devoted follower of Jesus Christ.

Yet in a letter written to believers in Rome, whom he had only met through correspondence, Paul poured out his soul. He exposed his most troubling challenges. As much as I want to stop, I continue to do these rotten things, Paul writes. I can't help myself. For some reason, the sin that lives in me is what I keep doing - not the good that I want to do.

Oh, dear Paul, you know my heart. You express my struggles. You say the words my soul yearns to articulate. I am not as brave as you, Paul, for I keep hiding these things in my life. My actions don't match my intentions. This is a blinding double standard with strong roots in my life.

While Paul spilled his guts nearly 2,000 years ago, are the 21st century struggles much different? Could Paul's words be your words? Did Paul struggle with some of the same underlying challenges as Martha?

Loading Up Our Plates

Too often, my daily schedule looks much like my dinner plate - heaping with more than I can chew. I eat with my eyes rather than my stomach. While I want bites that will nourish and energize my body, I gravitate towards calorie-laden foods filled with sugar. Any time I eat a salad and healthy foods, later, I allow myself to cheat just a bit... When I don't fit into my pants, I can only blame myself for the choices that I make.

Life is full of choices. We make them EVERY. SINGLE. DAY. Everything is a choice, even decisions we aren't aware of making. We bemoan constant activity, without acknowledging that we make choices about whether we engage in an activity or not.

For most Martha's, embracing the word "No" is so difficult. However, saying "Yes" to more work means saying "No" to a full night's sleep. Saying "Yes" to having a family means saying "No" to choices we made before having kids. Saying "Yes" to plopping down in front of the TV after a demanding day of work means saying "No" to feeding our bodies and souls with exercise or journaling or prayer.

When I have overindulged in a big meal, I feel awful. My tummy screams for relief. I vow to "know better" next time. Sometimes this works; sometimes it doesn't.

Willpower is only effective when I *choose* for it to work. Having an overfull life feels no better than an overstuffed stomach. Just like eating right, finding more Mary-ness in our Martha lives takes more than willpower. After a lifetime of making the same mistake over and over, it was time to acknowledge repetitious pitfalls. Only then could I reframe my Martha attitude.

Modern-Day Pitfalls for Many Martha's

Let's begin by identifying places where Martha's are often vulnerable. These situations are not an exhaustive list. They are some I see challenging myself and other Martha's.

Choosing the Urgent Over the Intentional

I can begin the day with the best intentions. When an unexpected email or phone call happens, suddenly, I find myself choosing a different path for the day than I had planned.

As a seemingly "urgent" request happens, it is easy to change a day's course without thinking about it. Whether we feel a responsibility to fulfill the request or we do not want to let someone down, we take on the task.

Choosing the urgent is always a choice. In prioritizing the new task, we determine that this new request is more important than anything else we had planned. We must see this as *our* choice, not someone else's. Before making a decision, determine whether or not the request is truly urgent. Is the unexpected interruption something that demands time and attention now? Or can the request be delayed until another time?

Hopping from one urgent task to another removes intentional decisions in our lives. Always choosing the urgent prevents us from making strides towards long-term goals and desires. Being intentional means saying "No" to some good things. It reinforces our need to choose only those things God calls us to do. The world will not stop if you say, "No."

Procrastination

Martha's love the adage, "If you want something done, ask a busy person." Yes, this is often true. I am more productive when I have more things to do. The pressure of looming deadlines spurs me to accomplish a lot.

Whether I have a full workload or not, procrastination creeps into my life. Even when I have lots to do, I find myself putting off a task. Maybe it's because this job isn't my favorite thing. Or I am tired and lack creative juices. Other times, my mind just wants to be numb and not think. I also know that, because I have pulled so many things together at the last minute, I can do this one more time.

Procrastination can be a Martha's best friend. It can also increase anxiety and anxiousness. I find it helpful to break big projects into smaller bites that I can complete more easily. This allows me to feel regular progress towards the larger goal. A little reward for completing something can also be motivating.

When I Get Organized, Things Will Be Better

I have bought many planners and calendars, hoping "this one" will finally get me organized. I have designed my own systems with clearly laid out goals and desires. These tools only work when I follow through.

It is easy for Martha's to focus on daily to-do lists and crossing off completed items, without fully integrating how what we do fits into a larger understanding of our life priorities. Unless we make time to identify and work towards goals and dreams, we'll be stuck in the cross-it-off-my-to-do-list mode forever.

Slow the Constant Negative Monologue Playing in Your Head

Often, there's a non-stop negative monologue that plays on repeat in my head. It exploits all the negative views I have of myself. This monologue is very draining and distracting.

The best way to slow the negative train is to replace it with helpful, positive thoughts. Encourage yourself rather than discourage yourself. Replace thoughts, beliefs, and habits that do not serve you well with thoughts, beliefs, and habits that will. Treat yourself kindly, like a good friend, instead of feeding the criticism tape. What would you tell a friend if they were in this spot?

Looking Somewhere Else for Affirmation

It's tempting to look at a crowd and let them tell us where we should be rather than making this assessment for ourselves. This isn't a bad thing, as long as the crowd is made up of Godly people who will encourage you in the right direction. Sometimes, "good enough" is as good as it gets. Be OK with this and move on.

Making Life's Plate More Manageable

Can struggling Martha's make progress towards more Mary-ness in their lives? Yes, with intention and grace. Here are a few ways I try to keep my life plate more manageable.

Make a Date with Yourself ... and Keep It

Until you grasp a true sense of your reality, nothing will change. Creating your own Mary Experiment will remain elusive. Set aside a chunk of time to make tough choices in your life. It may take more than one date to work through this.

Answer questions that may be hard. Hold yourself accountable for your choices. Create the best life God inspires for you. Unless you dig deep and are honest, you will continue to bite off more than you can chew.

Yes, your choices affect other people's lives. Only you determine if choices feel like you are following God in your life.

Here are some questions to help you start:

- What is God calling me to do with my life? Where is my sweet spot where my gifts and God's plans intersect?
- How can I surrender my best wishes and let God take ahold and work through me to bring me to the spot God has planned for me?
- What areas of my life do not clearly reflect the values and priorities that are most important to me?
- How will I handle feedback which does not line up with where I see God calling me in my life?

Design a Realistic Plan

After you have struggled with the big, life-changing questions, develop a plan. Our lives have many seasons. Previous choices influence our lives today. Developing a plan means honoring these commitments and choices while allowing God space to guide you forward.

This includes prioritizing steps. It's impossible to change everything at once. Break your plan into simple baby steps, which allow you to make quick progress and encourage you to stay on task. When you are comfortable with one change, then pursue another.

We usually assess how choices affect our family's calendar and finances, focusing on limited resources. I prefer to think of my time, talents, and finances as being more abundant than I could ever hope for. Generosity is not best assessed by our checkbooks and our calendars. It is a condition of our hearts. When we see the blessings in our lives as bestowed upon us by a generous God, we loosen the reins on our resources and release more of them into God's kingdom.

Simplify

I am regularly overwhelmed and embarrassed by the time spent managing our possessions. My goal is to be in a spot where I manage our possessions rather than allowing our possessions to manage me.

Simplifying involves more than getting rid of stuff. It also relates to our attitudes. Put little energy into things that carry little future relevance. If you will not be thinking about something in five weeks or five years, then you do not want to spend more than five minutes on it right now. Save your energy for the situations in life that require significant energy.

Build Empty Blocks to Create Moments of Mary Space in Your Daily Life

When schedules are too full and have little flexibility, we lose creativity. Section off blocks of unscheduled time. Blocks of down time. Blocks to have fun and make memories. Blocks to refresh yourself. Time to think, be, and reflect.

If finding empty blocks feels impossible, go through your plan and say "No" to more things. Or enlist others to help, with the promise that you will have more open opportunities. Then, keep your word. Refrain from adding in one more thing at the end of the day or filling up empty blocks with something someone deemed as urgent. Instead, plan life-giving and joy-granting leisure activities.

To find more Mary-ness, I find ways that encourage me to slow down and enjoy the moment. Begin by praying in bed before your feet hit the ground or you look at your phone. I use a simple prayer like this: "Dear God, thank you for this day. Walk with me through every hour. Help me make good choices that reflect Your call in my life. Grant me patience and wisdom as I encounter others. May we do this day together. Amen."

Identify other ways that you can slow your day down, if only for a moment:

- Read scripture, a daily devotional or a blog that centers your day.
- Express gratitude.
- Give yourself permission to not be perfect.
- Take care of your body. Feed your soul.
- Bookend your day with prayer in bed. Pray the Lord's Prayer as a way to close the day.

We can easily add these Mary-moments to our "to-do" checklist. Refrain from this. Let these moments be organic. Drop the expectation that something must be done every day.

Life is a Puzzle

Today, you have 1,440 minutes. Tomorrow, you will have another 1,440 minutes. This week, you will have 10,080 minutes. In a 30-day month, you will have 43,200 minutes. In the next year, you will have 525,600 minutes. You get to choose how you spend those minutes. You choose what priorities you have with each minute, day, week, and month.

Will I ever fully discover a rhythm of life where I am truly comfortable and content? Honestly, I don't think so. We cannot change how God has wired us. We can adjust our attitude and intentions. We can explore ways to live our lives with less heaping plates, only biting into the things of life which brings us closer to where God calls us to be. We can invite God to partner with us in making the hard choices and choosing our best life.

As I have journeyed towards creating a Mary Experiment in my life, maybe my most important discovery is this: God prefers that we live within some tension between Martha and Mary in our lives. When we allow for this tension, we give God space to bless us with an abundant life.

Often, we fantasize about living an extraordinary life. Here's the deal: When God is a part of our lives, we are ALREADY living an extraordinary life! God-sized dreams aren't about size at all. It's about what fits into your heart and choosing God's purpose for your life.

It's natural to look at someone else and think, "Wow. They're doing much bigger things than I am." God sees your life through a very different lens. The Almighty simply yearns for you to walk with the Lord. Ask for guidance. Consult with God repeatedly. Surround your life with the knowledge that the Alpha and the Omega has already smothered you with grace.

When we see ordinary things as being the most important things, our perspectives will shift. Like Paul, I pray we find peace and celebrate the times we make good choices. Yes, there will be days when our plates will continue to be heaping beyond control. There will be seasons when it will be impossible to keep all the balls in the air. But if we live according to God's plan for our lives, we can accept those, too, by staying focused on the things that truly matter. I pray we grant ourselves enough grace and mercy to celebrate the grace and mercy God extends us today.

Reflection Questions:

1. How often do you let the urgent take priority in your life? When you make an intentional choice for the day, is it easy or hard to sway from this choice?

2. Express your relationship with willpower. Is willpower easy for you or a constant struggle?

3. What is something in your life that you do, even though you would like to not do it?

4. Can you identify a pitfall that repeatedly happens in your life that prevents you from moving towards the life you envision?

5. Set a date with yourself to work through creating an intentional plan about the choices you prefer in your life.

Prayer:

Dear God – Forgive us for constantly piling more and more on our plates, with little intentional thought about whether or not we should include these things in our lives. Thank you for giving us an alternative to willpower. Help us take baby steps towards embracing this in our lives. Amen.

CHAPTER 14

When Life Falls Apart

He (Job) replied, "You are talking like a foolish woman. Shall we accept good from God, and not trouble?"

- Job 2:10a (NIV)

One fall, my quaint little world was turned upside down.

My friend Kristin teaches Spanish. She asked if I wanted to join her on a trip to Argentina, spurred by a continuing education scholarship she had received. My one condition was including a continuing education experience for me as well, which was accomplished by visiting an orphanage.

On the day of our departure, my younger sister Debbie called. My dad had chronic obstructive pulmonary disease (COPD). He was in the hospital for additional pulmonary treatments to ease his breathing. Dad encouraged me to continue with the planned trip.

Kristin and I shared American culture with Argentinian students at several schools; their witty questions and inquisitive minds kept us entertained.

We noticed a significantly different environment at the orphanage that we visited. The kids desperately needed the clothes, school supplies, candy, and crafts we brought with us. They were enthralled making simple holiday crafts, as well as cross necklaces and bracelets. One little girl made the same cross necklace three times and proudly asked me to tie each one around her neck.

While cleaning up, I gathered the left-over sticker sheets for the garbage. A teenaged girl asked if she could have a sticker sheet with only a couple stickers left on it. My heart nearly broke as she explained that she wanted something just for herself.

Before leaving the orphanage, we gave the kids candy. We took the leftovers into the kitchen to ask the cook to parcel it out over the next several days. The cook grabbed our hands and expressed deep gratitude for our visit. She said our presence made a huge difference and called us heroes. Kristin told the woman that her daily presence with the kids made her their real hero.

As we returned to the states, my spiritual temperature was soaring. Kristin and I felt a great sense of contribution and accomplishment. I noted stories that I could use as sermon illustrations. I contemplated how lessons learned from this trip could translate into our local community.

Then, reality hit. While my dad was finally home from the hospital, Mom was now at the hospital with cellulitis. The next day, my mother-in-law Ersel was admitted as well. It was time to accurately assess her declining health.

The next six weeks were a blur. My mother-in-law was moved to a nursing home. One of my parents would make it home from the hospital, only to have the other parent return the next day. With treatment options exhausted, it was time for my dad to enroll in Hospice. Christmas was just around the corner. Dad opted to stay at a nursing home for two weeks before returning home for his last days. A couple days before Christmas, we celebrated with my parents. Everyone present knew this was Dad's last Christmas.

As a pastor, December is filled with Advent and Christmas services and celebrations. Somehow, they all came together - often at the last minute, glued together between trips to the hospital, nursing homes, and our parents' homes.

On Christmas Day, my mother-in-law was rushed to the hospital with significant internal bleeding. Still emotionally drained from the Christmas celebration at my parents and Christmas Eve services, Rick and I felt worn out and exhausted. With the bleeding under control, Ersel was moved to ICU. Rick was scheduled to work, so I spent the night at the hospital. For the first time in weeks, I just sat. My exhausted soul could not handle one more thing. I couldn't contemplate what HAD to be done tomorrow.

The next morning, Mom was back in the hospital. The cellulitis had quickly spread overnight. Dad was moving home that day. If Ersel was stable, how soon could I come and help?

The next week, I spent as much time with my dad as I could, while finding moments to be with my mom and mother-in-law. I had gone home for 24-hours when the call came that I needed to return to my parents' house immediately. The end was near. Rick and I sped back to my parents. Throughout the day, Dad slept. He woke up in the evening, hungry for a grilled cheese sandwich. After a couple bites, he asked Rick to eat the rest. He swung his legs back into bed and fell asleep.

I stayed up with Dad that night, keeping him comfortable, holding his hand, retelling favorite stories, and sharing what he meant to me. When the Hospice nurse arrived the next morning, our family friend, Celeste, was also there. As Celeste, the nurse, and I stood around his bed, my dad quietly and calmly slipped away.

While my Martha-ness wanted me to hold everything together, my heart could barely process the range of emotions from the previous intense weeks. The tension of being wired as a Martha while yearning for some contemplative Mary-ness in my life was terribly acute. As a pastor, I have journeyed with countless families through their emotional, physical, and spiritual roller coasters. Finding yourself on such a ride and not knowing how to properly navigate the turns is extremely humbling. Would these life experiences challenge me to rethink how my Martha tendencies impact how I lived my life?

Blaming God

As a pastor, the questions I most often field relate to God "causing" bad things to happen to people. How could a loving God yank a child away from a parent? If God can do anything, why would God allow awful natural disasters to rip people's lives apart? Why does God seem to answer the prayers of some, but not others?

My answers to all of these questions, and many more, are highly inadequate. My belief system says that God does not cause every awful thing that happens in this world. Evil does. Why God allows evil to seemingly take over and perpetuate in certain instances, I have no answer. I can only trust that the Lord's intentions will be made known at the proper time.

My faith system tells me that when I walk through intense times and my life feels like it is falling apart, I never journey alone. God is always, always, always with me. Even when the Lord is not taking the action I would prefer, or when I am angry and upset, the Almighty still hangs in the shadows of my life. The Holy One is just waiting to be called upon to shower me with grace, compassion, and comfort. I cannot adequately answer the "Why did this happen?" or "Where is God now?" questions. What I *can* share is the knowledge of who walks beside us in the darkest valleys of life. It's the same One who celebrates every joy and happiness we have ever embraced.

Everything Doesn't Happen for a Reason

If I could remove one platitude from the English language, it would be this one: *Everything happens for a reason.* When we say this statement, do we really believe that people get raped and beaten for a reason? Does God cause people to be killed when their vehicle is hit by a drunk driver? When a child dies of leukemia, do we really believe God just wants another angel in heaven?

I do not find this statement comforting. Theologically, it raises all kinds of problems. I do not believe God intended for 9.11.2001 to happen. An awful, tragic event happened because sinful people planned it.

Romans 8:28 is often quoted when trying to make sense of God's trials:

> *And we know that God causes everything to work together for the good of those who love God and are called according to his purpose for them.*
>
> **– Romans 8:28 (NLT)**

Look carefully at what Paul says. It does not say that everything that happens is good. It says that the Lord is at work in all things, and God's purpose will not be undermined by evil.

Assuming that everything happens for a reason lumps together what God allows and what the Lord causes -

what God permits and what the Lord prefers. It's unfair to blame the Almighty for bad choices or assume the Holy One will fix every poor decision. Instead, God promises to continue working for eternal good, no matter how many short-sighted decisions sinful people make. Likewise, I do not believe God never gives you more than you can handle. Rather, the Lord longs to be with us when our lives are overflowing and out-of-control.

What would be a more appropriate response when someone is struggling? Share that you are thinking and praying for them. Express that you do not have words to say and give them a long hug.

Lessons from Job

In the Bible, Job has the difficult task of presenting a healthy way to understand disappointment and grief. While his "friends" encourage him to turn away from God, Job is steadfast in his commitment, even as his life fell apart. He states his case: if we are willing to accept God's goodness, troubles will be part of the deal. It's a lesson he has unfortunately been dealt, one he wishes God would explain to him.

Accepting the lesson Job embraced is incredibly difficult. When life falls apart, we want to hold someone accountable. The simplest culprit is God. However, the Almighty does not guarantee Christians will not travel through dark valleys in their lives. The Lord will not patch up everyone's mistakes. When God chooses not to fix something, getting angry only distances us from the Holy One. Even if we are upset with the Lord, God longs to journey with us through life's darkest valleys.

When life is falling apart, our souls need grace. Compassion. Peace. In the thick of awful times in our lives, our best response is to cradle ourselves within God's hands and discover the Lord's grace. When we allow our hearts to move to this place, then we open ourselves to know the Holy One at a deeper level. God longs for us to show up with a battered and beaten heart, to sit at the Lord's feet and allow healing. Like Mary, our most important spot is to sit as close to Jesus as we can.

In the weeks preceding my dad's death, trying to have a "normal" existence was impossible. I could only focus on what needed to be done in the moment to make it through the day. Quiet time with God only happened while driving from one crisis to the next.

Embracing some Mary-ness in my life seemed elusive. Most of the time, I felt like my only option was to do. Yet, in the midst of all the chaos, there were times when I could just be. Unfortunately, I didn't fully realize these opportunities until I looked back and saw them as mini-respites in the midst of chaos. It happened as I sat curled up in a hospital chair while sitting with Ersel on Christmas night. As I watched the snow fall outside the hospital window, I realized that holding my dad's hand during his final hours was truly a gift.

When life happens and you feel swallowed up in the moment, I pray you can allow yourself to slow down, step back, and try to contemplate God's desire for you in the moment. Be angry with God if you must. I pray Job's demeanor and Mary's example will encourage you to not turn completely away from God.

Letting Go of Perfect

When it feels like life is falling apart around you, please stop. Let go of trying to be Ms. Perfect-Martha-Pants. Hang onto the fact that Jesus *loved* Martha. Jesus *loves* you. The Lord does not require a perfect version of yourself to receive God's grace. Let go of the notion that you must be perfect in order for the Almighty, others, or yourself to accept you. Perfect is not what God desires. The Lord simply desires an open heart that shows up and is ready to be molded. As the Holy One forgives you unconditionally, be forgiving of yourself.

Learning from Life's Lessons

It took a while before I could fully process all that happened in those six weeks between Thanksgiving and into the New Year. It would take a few more life lessons before I could fully come to grips with a deeper need to create a Mary Experiment in my life. Yet, as God continued to work in my heart, I discovered a stronger demand for less doing and more being in my life. I was also confident that God would journey with me as I continued through this discovery process.

Reflection Questions:

1. Identify a time in your life when you felt your life crumbling apart. How did you respond? Did you do, be, or simply want to hide?
2. When something awful happens, God often receives the blame. Job's friends advocated for this. Why do you think Job was so convinced God should not be blamed?
3. Jesus *loved* Martha. Jesus *loves* you. How does this affect your view of when bad things happen in your life?

Prayer:

Holy God – Please forgive me for all the times I quickly blamed You for something awful that happened. Allow me to see alternatives. May Job inspire me to not give up on You, but simply be with You. Amen.

CHAPTER 15

A Long-Term Recovering Martha

Always be full of joy in the Lord. I say it again—rejoice! Let everyone see that you are considerate in all you do. Remember, the Lord is coming soon. Don't worry about anything; instead, pray about everything. Tell God what you need and thank Him for all He has done. Then you will experience God's peace, which exceeds anything we can understand. His peace will guard your hearts and minds as you live in Christ Jesus.

- Philippians 4:4-7 (NLT)

Going car shopping with Hubby Rick is a trip. He considers car shopping an experience. He can look and look and look at cars. Picking a car should not be rushed. This is a multiple-year investment that demands lots of testing and evaluating. Even if the exterior looks flashy and the paint color is cool, he always opens the hood and looks inside. The nuts and bolts of the car – the motor, transmission, and other working parts – are super important.

By contrast, his Martha-minded wife simply wants to find a car, make the deal, and drive off the lot. Rick wants to slide under the car and check out the muffler. He sticks a penny into the tire and evaluates how much tread there is. He reminds me that he can't buy anything without "sleeping on it."

Imagine my surprise when we found ourselves making a deal to buy a different vehicle within an hour of driving onto the car lot. It was not our intent to even look at cars that day, let alone buy one...

Why was Rick able to make a quick decision that day? Because we knew exactly what we were looking for. It was the same make and model as another car we have, just a later year with fewer miles. I don't need a flashy vehicle - just a dependable one. Amazingly, Rick shook hands on the deal, and we were leaving the car lot before I could process it all.

On the way home, I contemplated how different this midsize SUV is from the flashy Corvette Rick drove during our dating days. His all-white 1977 Corvette had T-tops, wide rear tires, one spoiler under the front bumper and another on the rear trunk. Nearly every time Rick drove this Corvette, someone would toot their horn or roll down their window and tell him what a nice car it was.

Our Flashy Hoods

While Rick's car looked great at a glance, with a little deeper inspection, little flaws exposed themselves. There were cracks in the maroon vinyl seats. The floor carpet showed wear. While it could go zero to very fast in no time at all and sounded boss, my short legs never reached the gas pedal comfortably. Behind the wheel, I felt like I was three inches off of the pavement - not a selling point for me. Rick knew his car could be a chick magnet... but not for me. I was more than happy with a reliable and realistic ride.

Often, we want our lives to look like the flashy Corvette. It's not uncommon for some people to put lots of effort into making sure their outside appearance is just as flashy as a sports car. Perfectly styled hair and a great make-up job will not eternally camouflage hidden pain and discomfort. Fitting into the latest skinny jeans or fashionable yoga pants does not guarantee a happy life.

We often use the hoods of our lives to try and hide what is really going on. Stress and financial worries can cause a person's life to crack and rust. Years of unhealthy habits show up as exterior wear. Constantly trying to keep up with everyone else and not being content with your own life manifests itself as bald tires trying to burn through life.

When Martha's endlessly try to be something other than themselves, they eventually become exhausted. People not content with their current stage of life put too much effort into the wrong things. Running on fumes with little self-care or quiet time leads to having a life that may look great... but soon leads to burn out.

Car aficionados love to find a 'diamond in the rough' vehicle and restore it to its former glory. They want the outside and the inside to look fabulous. Sometimes, it may feel like our lives need that kind of complete overhaul. We think, "Oh, if only ..." With any amount of life responsibilities or commitments, going through a complete overhaul is usually not realistic. There must be an alternative.

I am convinced that change can happen right where you are, in any stage of your life. You don't have to stop everything to discover the life you've always wanted. Love your life today, and you can become excited with your future. Commit to making a few tweaks over time and you CAN discover and become the best version of yourself.

An Unfinished Story

To me, the Martha and Mary story ends abruptly. After Jesus encourages Martha to focus less on what she sees as her priorities and be open to shifting her perspective, we never hear Martha's response. I wish Martha's words were included in the story. Did she accept Jesus' redirection and encouragement? Could Martha allow herself to make small tweaks in her daily life so that she could find more contentment and peace? Or did she continue to struggle with her Type A personality forever?

Unfortunately, we do not know the answers to these questions. Yet, the author of Luke's gospel felt this story was important enough that he included it in his account of Jesus' life. It was a message early Christian believers needed to hear. Our need to heed this story is no less significant today.

Living Your Best Life Today

As a woman who now has lived over a half-of-a-century (gasp!), I have the opportunity to look in the rearview mirror of my life. I have tried to embrace the life lessons as they have showed up. Other times, I completely missed them, or did not think they applied to me. How silly I was!

With hopefully a bit more wisdom than my younger self, I've been picking out the most important things for me to focus on in this stage of my life. What these priorities look like will be different at various stages of life. Priorities of your 20's will be different from the priorities of your 30's, 40's, 50's and so on. Today, I hope that I embrace the life teachings that my younger self did not understand. With more self-awareness and humility, I have learned from previous experiences which will hopefully save me a few steps in the future.

In my early 30's, I found myself with the opportunity to make a new choice in my life. I left a job that I loved, in order to climb the corporate ladder. A year later, the new job did not work out. Instead of climbing, I hit a ceiling. Jobless, I was 30, unmarried with no children or debt. While I was not wealthy, I could choose to do whatever I wanted next. I was at a crossroads.

I was also nearing the end of an intensive 34-week Bible study. While I had been raised attending and participating in church since forever, this Bible study literally rocked my world. For the first time ever, I truly read the Bible. I now saw the entire Bible as part of a larger meta narrative that transcended time. While the Bible is the story of God, the Lord's people and the Almighty's Son, Jesus, I now saw myself as part of the extended story. The message of God's unconditional love for people undergirded each week's reading. In scripture, I saw a new opportunity. I wanted this narrative story to be part of my life forever.

How do you see God as part of your story? How are you part of God's story?

I began looking for opportunities to spend a year overseas while serving God. As I explored being a missionary for a year, I took a test designed to help people discover how they might serve in ministry overseas. I was disappointed with receiving only one suggested match: teaching English.

Seriously? Only one match? I had a choice: I could be frustrated, or I could embrace it. I signed up to serve overseas as an English teacher for one school year, which included six weeks of training. Halfway through the training, I would know where I would be placed.

As part of the placement process, we were placed with another teacher, with whom we would live and teach. We were assured we would be sent either to our top geographical choices or with teachers we felt compatible with.

I was mad when neither of these were honored in my situation. Through this process, I had carefully followed and trusted God's leading. I had been faithful. This was my reward?

At the time, my immature faith was not as solid and developed as Job's faith. I wanted to negotiate with God, even though I knew this was impossible. It took some discernment, trust, and relaxation of my strong-willed Martha attitude to get on a plane with a final destination of Almaty, Kazakhstan.

Thank goodness I did. As I explored a new culture, I discovered that strong Martha personalities were not applauded after decades of communist rule. Many of the students could literally pack all of their possessions into smaller suitcases than the two I had brought with me. I began to appreciate a slower and more thoughtful life pace. While teaching students about Western American culture, I discovered that I had as much to learn as they did.

God's sense of humor was not lost on me. At the end of the school year, the strong-willed Martha person who arrived was not the same person returning to America.

Back in the States, I vowed not to return to some of my previous lifestyle habits and choices. Yet, quickly, my Martha-like tendencies re-emerged. While Mary had found a bit of herself within me in Almaty, back in my culture, she was relegated to the back seat of the car, told to cover up with a blanket, and take a long nap.

She stayed there for a long time until I become serious about letting Mary find a little more footing in my life. Honestly, the struggle has been consistent and ongoing. While I often internally yearned for more Mary in my life, my application sucked. It has caused me to often question whether I could ever really become a long-term recovering Martha with more Mary in my life.

The Mary Experiment

When I began the Mary Experiment, it was not a book. It was a journey, an opportunity for me to see whether I could set aside some of my overarching Martha tendencies and find more contentment, peace, and quiet in my day-to-day life.

As I have continued on this experiment, I have learned several life lessons. Some days, the Mary Experiment feels more possible than others. I am not sure there will ever be a day when I feel like I have adequately crossed everything off of my to-do list. However, at times I can be more realistic about what is possible within a certain timeframe.

I allow for grace. Rather than setting myself up for failure by expecting myself to do something every day of the week, I celebrate the days that I was able to exercise, or go on a walk with Hubby Rick, or have desired quiet time with God. Some days, if I can accomplish a couple of those ideal things, I call it good enough and challenge myself to be at peace.

Over time, I've seen that God's call in my life has been changing constantly. Just because God desired for me to serve God's kingdom in one particular way for a season, does not guarantee this will be my life's call forever. Moving into a new phase can be intimidating. When I am confident this evolution is rooted in God's call for me, I walk into the unknown with contentment.

Regularly, I still yearn for a boring day - a day when I can simply goof off. When this thought becomes too persistent, I remind myself that every day, I *choose* what I do. If I want something different, it's up to me to consult with God and figure this out.

I challenge myself to live in and celebrate the gift of today. We can put lots of energy and worry into what is going to happen tomorrow. As much as I like to plan and anticipate, I am discovering that focusing too much on tomorrow keeps me from being still today. I try to occupy today without extending too much worry or concern about tomorrow and the future. If I keep God next to me, we will tackle whatever comes my way.

I'm trying to drop my superhero cape and be comfortable with just being Dianne. I'm discovering that what God thinks of me is far more important than what other people think of me. I long to be comfortable with a mediocre life, one in which simply being who I am is enough. My enough will not be based on someone else's measuring stick of whether I am spiritual enough. Or Christian enough. Or whether or not my marriage is good enough. I hope that I can embrace my shortcomings, rather than constantly justifying or making excuses for them.

Your Perfect Day

In his book *Tuesdays with Morrie*, author Mitch Albom asks his beloved professor, Morrie Schwatrz, what he would do if he had one 24-hour perfectly healthy day. Morrie struggled with ALS and had limited physical capabilities. He shared how he would get up in the morning, do his exercises, have a lovely breakfast of sweet rolls and tea, go for a swim, then have his friends over for a nice lunch. He'd have them come one or two at a time so they could talk about their families, their issues, and about how much they mean to each other. Then he'd go for a walk in a garden with some trees, enjoy their colors, watch the birds, take in the nature that he hadn't seen in such a long time. Finally, in the evening, he would go to a restaurant with great pasta and maybe some duck, and dance the rest of the night. He'd dance until he was exhausted, then slip into a deep, wonderful sleep.

Mitch was surprised by how simple Morrie would make his day. Actually, he was a little disappointed that Morrie didn't want to fly to Italy, or have lunch with the President, or romp along the seashore, or try every exotic thing he could think of. After days of not being able to move a foot or a leg, how could he find perfection in such an average day?

"Then I realized, this was the whole point," Albom writes.

More than once, I have contemplated what my perfect day would look like. It would include devotions in my reading chair with a cup of Highlander Grog coffee. I'd chat with a dear friend over a great lunch of a crisp lettuce salad, slightly covered with a dressing and all my favorite toppings, and chased down with gallons of cold peach iced tea. Later, Hubby Rick and I would go for a hike or bike ride, and stop along the way to simply smell the air. We'd talk nonstop about nothing and everything. After dinner at a table filled with candles and great food, I'd take a long bath, filled to the brim with bubbles, and know that it had been a good day.

What would your perfect day look like? What would you want to include? What would be necessary for you to declare that it had been a good day?

As I have navigated this Mary Experiment, I have discovered that I do not have to wait for the perfect day to do these things. I can embrace these things today. I won't be able to make every day a completely perfect day, but I can include bits and pieces of my perfect day in my life every week. It's my choice.

Do you feel the need to wait for the perfect day to do some of those things today? Or can you discover ways to embrace them now? These choices are ones you can make.

Embrace God's calling in your life. Live life not just with a flashy hood and colorful paint job, but embracing the values, qualities, and personality God has gifted you with. Rejoice for the good days AND the challenging days. Embrace prayer as a way for God to change you into your best version. Remember that *Whose* you are is just as important as *who* you are. Repeatedly, embrace every blessing in your life, be grateful that God has more sense than you do - the sense to gift you with blessings that you may not think you need. Accept that some blessings you yearn for may not be part of your plan. Finally, keep yourself grounded in Jesus, who loved Martha, who loved Mary, and who definitely loves you.

Your Mary Experiment

There was a reason why you picked up this book and began reading it. Maybe there was a reason someone handed you a copy of the story of my struggle to chase a Mary Experiment in my life.

Now, it's your turn to continue to develop your own Mary Experiment. Life is your opportunity to consult with God about God's dream for your life and your spot in God's kingdom. You choose how the words of my story resonate with your story. You determine whether or not the things of your past will influence how you live your life today. It's up to you whether or not a personal Mary Experience will bring focus to the daily choices that you make. You decide when it's time to *do*, and when you need to simply *be*.

Reflection Questions:

1. Reflect upon your current life story. What parts of your history are most important to you today? What has your younger version discovered that you want to embrace today?

2. How do you see yourself as part of God's story? How will you continue the story God has granted you with today? Tomorrow?

3. What will you do to continue to finish your story strong?

4. How important is having a Mary Experiment in your life to you? Set a date with yourself within the next week to continue exploring your Mary Experiment. Determine a time when you can weekly continue evaluating your Mary Experiment.

5. Give thanks to God for the life you have. Pray for God to continue to be a part of your journey every day going forward.

Prayer:

Dear God – I pray that I can truly be amazed by this life that You have given me. I pray that I view every day as a gift, a present, that I will embrace. Please continue to be a part of my daily journey. Encourage me to find a little Mary in my life today and again tomorrow. May we work together to build a continual Mary Experiment that helps keep me at Your feet. Amen.

Acknowledgments

When I began contemplating turning my Mary Experiment into a book, several ladies participated in two focus groups. There, we explored the feelings real-life Martha's deal with on a daily basis. From these focus groups, I received the encouragement and initial material to begin crafting *The Mary Experiment*.

Thanks to the ladies who joined these focus groups: Myhia Chapman, Eleanor Engelby, Sara Ludtke, Liz Nelson, Mindy Roth, Heather Snyder, Kelly Trudell, Pam Wentz, and Jo Wheeler. You ladies provide the encouragement for me to move forward with this project.

During one of these focus groups, the ladies insisted that they wanted to be part of the book's journey. A few more women joined this group. Some of them call this group The Book Club. Some call it The God Squad. I called it my Focus Group. No matter what the title, these ladies provided honest and invaluable feedback. They critiqued each chapter, provided feedback on the entire book, and held me accountable by always setting our next meeting time. Because this Martha did not want to show up with no chapters to review, this group helped me cross the finish line. I'm not sure we were ever all together at the same time. Yet, each one of you offered suggestions and insights which have only improved the finished product. Thanks for being

Martha and Mary's who supported me through this process! You ladies rock!

The God Squad ladies include: Myhia Chapman, Sarah Danz, Eleanor Engelby, Carrie Louis, Sara Ludtke, Liz Nelson, Mindy Roth and Linda Weber.

Thank you to the women who assisted me in the final drafting of the book: editor Nicole Smith, formatter Rachel Cox and book designer Tara Kindschi.

About The Author

Hard-working. Dependable. Consistent. Reliable.

These words appropriately describe Dianne Deaton Vielhuber. Raised on a small Wisconsin dairy farm, her parents instilled within her these and other traditional Midwest values. On their family farm, work was never considered a dirty word, and everyone was expected to pitch in. She earned a Bachelor of Science degree from the University of Wisconsin-Madison in Agricultural Journalism. After working in communications and marketing within agriculture for many years, she felt called to serve overseas as a missionary. After a life-changing year teaching English at a university in Almaty, Kazakhstan, Dianne returned to the United States. She expected to return to the business world. Rather, God called her into pastoral ministry. Dianne earned a Master of Divinity from the University of Dubuque Theological Seminary while serving as a student pastor. In 20 years, she served five different United Methodist churches as a part of three appointments within the Wisconsin Annual Conference.

Ordained an elder within the United Methodist Church, Dianne now yearns for new words to accurately describe her: Grounded in God. Relatable. Practical faith journey. Assisting others to journeying with God daily.

She writes regularly for her blog, *Simple Words of Faith*, where she explores finding God in everyday aspects of life. Her writing is grounded in real-life examples of how God desires to be part of our daily lives.

Dianne journeys through her life with Hubby Rick. They have six grandchildren, along with Rick's adult children. A self-proclaimed recovering over-doing Martha, Dianne incorporates Mary-like attitudes in her life through gardening, reading, and exercising. With Rick, they find satisfaction in remodeling a 110-year-old Victorian farmhouse in south-central Wisconsin.

Please follow Dianne at www.simplewordsoffaith.com and join the Simple Words of Faith Facebook community. Dianne can be reached at dideaton@hotmail.com.

Can You Help?

Thank You For Reading My Book!

I appreciate feedback. I would love to hear what you have to say about *The Mary Experiment: When DOING and BEING Collide.*

This will help improve the next version of this book and my future books.

Please leave me an honest review on Amazon, letting me know what you thought of the book.

Thanks so much!

Blessings -

Dianne Deaton Vielhuber

Made in the USA
San Bernardino, CA
30 January 2020